SECOND EDITION

How to Pass

D1338864

NATIONAL 5

English

David Swinney

HODDER GIBSON
AN HACHETTE UK COMPANY

Dedication: For Chloe and Hannah

The Publishers would like to thank the following for permission to reproduce copyright material:

Photo credits P.11 © Kari Tuomi/REX/Shutterstock; **p.27** © REX/Shutterstock; **p.34** © FotoJagodka - stock.adobe.com; **p.37** © David Caudery/Future Publishing/REX/Shutterstock; **p.45** © Jonathan Hordle/REX/Shutterstock; **p.60** © nickolae/Fotolia.com; **p.69** © Moviestore Collection/REX/Shutterstock; **p.72** © TSPL/Writer Pictures; **p.99** © Traverse Theatre

Acknowledgements P.3–4 extract from Franz Kafka, *The Trial*, translated by Willa and Edwin Muir (Penguin Books, 1953); **p.6** extract from Stephen Krashen, 'Wide reading is the key' from *The Guardian* (30 July, 2012), copyright Guardian News & Media Ltd 2018; **pp.9, 19** extracts from George Orwell, 'Politics and the English Language' (1946) from *Collected Essays, Journalism and the Letters of George Orwell* (Penguin Books, 1970); **pp.11–12** extract from Tove Jansson, 'Moonlight' from *The Summer Book* (Sort of Books, 2003) © Tove Jansson, 1972, Moomin Characters™ (Translation from Swedish © Thomas Teal, 2003); **pp.21–22** extract from 'Wages: Carer, banker, footballer: who really deserves the big bucks?', adapted from *The Observer* (16 July 2017), copyright Guardian News & Media Ltd 2018; **pp.23–24** extract from Tim Soutphommasane, 'In praise of … Paddington Bear' from *The Guardian* (2 June, 2008), copyright Guardian News & Media Ltd 2018; **pp.27–28** extract from Carole Cadwalladr, 'What drives Jessica Ennis?' from *The Observer* (4 November, 2012), copyright Guardian News & Media Ltd 2018; **p.32** extract adapted from Luc Sante, *Low Life: Lures and Snares of Old New York* (Farrar, Straus and Giroux, 1991) copyright © 1991 by Luc Sante. Reprinted by permission of The Joy Harris Literary Agency, Inc.; **pp.35–37** extract from D T Max, 'A Whole New Ball Game', adapted from *The New Yorker* (16 May 2016), copyright D T Max; **pp.45–47** extract from Emine Saner, 'The Saturday interview: Dynamo', adapted from *The Guardian* (7 July, 2012), copyright Guardian News & Media Ltd 2018; **pp.52–54** extract from Barbara McMahon, 'The iPaddy', adapted from *The Times* (26 March, 2013), copyright The Times/News Syndication; **pp.61, 78** extracts from SQA N5 English Critical Reading Specimen Paper, copyright © Scottish Qualifications Authority (n.b. answers do not emanate from SQA); **p.70** extract from Harper Lee, *To Kill a Mockingbird* (J.B. Lippincott & Co., 1960); **pp.73, 76–77, 81, 85–86** Norman MacCaig, 'Basking Shark' and 'Assisi' from *The Many Days: Selected Poems of Norman MacCaig* (Polygon, 2011), reproduced with permission of Birlinn Limited via PLSclear; **pp. 94–95** extract from Ann Marie di Mambro *Tally's Blood* (Hodder Gibson, 2014), reprinted by permission of Ann Marie di Mambro/MacFarlane Chard Associates.

SCOTLAND EXCEL

We are an approved supplier on the Scotland Excel framework.

Schools can find us on their procurement system as:

Hodder & Stoughton Limited t/a Hodder Gibson.

Contents

Introduction

The aim of this book is to help you to do well in National 5 English. You can read it, and work through the activities, on your own or with the help of someone else. It is aimed directly at the exam, but includes support for your coursework too. The exam comes at the end of your course of study, and tests your knowledge and understanding, as well as the skills you have learned. The exam is not meant to trick you or catch you out. It can't test you on everything you have learned throughout the year in English, it can only sample the different areas of the course. In the exam you will be given the chance to show what you have learned and how your skills have improved. There is nothing to be afraid of! As long as you know what you will be asked to do in the exam, and have done some preparation, you will be fine.

What you should know: National 5 English

The exam has two papers, Reading for Understanding, Analysis and Evaluation, and Critical Reading. There are two additional elements (the Portfolio–writing and the Performance–spoken language), that are not done in the exam. You are given time throughout the year to work on the Portfolio, and to demonstrate your skills in spoken language. Once your Portfolio of writing is completed, your teacher will send it to the SQA to be marked. Your teacher will assess your skills in spoken language. There are no marks or grades for this element: it is assessed 'achieved', or 'not achieved'. It is worth pointing out that the word 'Performance' does not mean that have to be judged on just one event. Your teacher can assess you over several occasions. A presentation in front of the class is not an essential requirement for this, a group discussion is perfectly acceptable.

Reading for Understanding, Analysis and Evaluation

In this paper you will be given a passage of text to read; it will be non-fiction and roughly 1,000 words in length. You will be asked approximately nine questions on the text. You will have one hour to do this, and the questions are worth 30 marks.

Chapters 3 and 4 of this book will help you with this. Chapter 4 includes three full exam papers for you to practise your skills, and provides the answers to all the questions, plus advice on how to find the answers and how to answer the questions effectively.

Critical Reading

There are two sections in this paper: questions on Scottish Texts and the Critical Essay.

In the Scottish Texts section you will be given an extract from all the Scottish texts that are selected for study by SQA. (An up-to-date list of these texts is on the SQA website.) You will have studied at least one of the Scottish writers from the list with your teacher. You are guaranteed a question on the writer you have studied. What you don't know before the exam is exactly which extracts will be chosen for the exam paper. This means that you have to study all of the texts by your chosen writer that appear on the list. You have to be able to answer the questions on the extract, but you also have to be able to answer a final question which asks you to compare the extract with other aspects of the writer's work. There are 20 marks in total for these questions. In Chapter 6 we shall look at two of the most popular Scottish writers on the list (the poet Norman MacCaig and the dramatist Ann Marie Di Mambro) to show how this assessment works in practice.

In the Critical Essay section, you will be given a selection of essay questions. You have to choose one question and write a critical essay on one of the literature, media or language texts you have studied as part of your course. You are not allowed to bring the texts you have studied into the exam – you have to work from memory. The essay you write is marked out of 20. The Critical Essay is dealt with in Chapter 5.

The Portfolio

The Portfolio is a mini collection of two pieces of your writing that has to be submitted a few weeks before your exam. Each piece is worth up to 15 marks, and these marks are added to the marks you achieve in the exam (up to 70), giving you a total out of 100.

You have to work on, and hand in, two pieces of writing. One should be what is called 'broadly creative'. This means that it can be a piece of personal writing (often called personal/reflective), in which you think and write about something in your life that has affected you in a big way; or it can be a piece of creative writing in which you create something using your imagination (a story, or part of a drama script, or a poem, for example).

The other piece of writing has to come under the heading of 'broadly discursive'. This means that it is essentially a mix of facts and opinions. You will be dealing with research, information and ideas in your preparation for this piece of writing.

The Portfolio is really something outwith the exam, but it counts towards your final mark. You will be working on this in class throughout your year of study, but Chapter 2 offers some help and advice on how to do well with it.

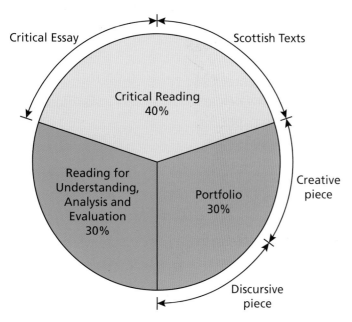

How the marks add up.

How the marks add up:
- Reading for Understanding, Analysis and Evaluation – 30 marks
- Critical Reading – 40 marks
  - Critical Essay – 20 marks
  - Scottish Texts – 20 marks
- Portfolio – 30 marks
  - Creative piece – 15 marks
  - Discursive piece – 15 marks
- Performance–spoken language – achieved/not achieved (0 marks)

National 4

National 4 English covers many of the same skills as National 5, and following the advice in this book will help you with what you have to do for National 4. There are a few things to note, however.

First of all, there is no exam at National 4. Instead there is the Added Value unit, which is an assignment or project that allows you to demonstrate your understanding of the key skills of the course. Then there is the Literacy unit. The Literacy unit is built into National 4 and it acts, in a way, like an extra qualification. A qualification in Literacy tells an employer or a college entrance officer that you are competent in the skills of reading, writing, talking and listening at National 4 level. The coursework and the assessments for Literacy will be based more on what is called 'functional English' than literature. The texts you study for Literacy (the ones you read or listen to) will be information-related rather than imaginative literature.

You can still take the Literacy unit at National 5, but it is an extra. You don't have to have the Literacy unit to pass the course.

How to pass English National 5

As I said above, this book will concentrate mainly on the National 5 English exam. It is designed so you can pick it up at any time during the course, read some of the advice and try some of the activities. You can dip in and out of the chapters as you come across things in the course that you are not sure about.

As the exam approaches, you have to try to get yourself in the right frame of mind to tackle it. It may well be one of the first proper exams you have taken, and you may be worried about how to prepare properly. Hopefully this book will reassure you about some of the things you find challenging.

Maybe you find the Reading for Understanding, Analysis and Evaluation part of the exam tricky. I have tried to give as much advice as I can about how to answer the kind of questions you'll face in this exam.

I mentioned trying to get yourself in the right frame of mind to tackle the exam. A lot of people panic as exams approach, and as a result don't manage to revise as well as they might because they are too anxious. Try to approach revision as calmly as you can. The box below gives some advice that might help you to revise for English (and your other subjects). I hope it works for you. Good luck!

Hints & tips

✓ *Don't surround yourself with lots of books and pages and pages of notes. Try to condense your notes so that you are left looking at fewer pieces of paper the closer you get to the exam. Doing this will force you to make decisions about what is really important and what is not. You can't remember everything, so it is best to remember the important stuff.*

✓ *Space out your key points on the paper you are working from.*

✓ *Try to write/highlight key points in different colours so they stand out.*

✓ *Concept maps. Concept maps. Concept maps.*

✓ *Try making mini posters of key points (maybe quotes to learn, and so on). Put them up in your room or around the house. Just seeing them every time you walk past will help you remember them (this really works!).*

✓ *When on study leave, make sensible use of your time: get up reasonably early; get some fresh air (go for a walk or jog, or offer to go for a pint of milk); be at your desk before 10 a.m.; work in sessions. Do something completely different at some point in the day to give your brain a break: read a book, play some football, play the guitar, ride your bike, or (if you must!) have a game or two on your games console.*

Good luck!

Chapter 1
Course content – making a start

What you should know

As I said in the introduction, for National 5 English there is an exam containing two question papers, one Portfolio (writing), and one Performance (spoken language).

The aim of the National 5 English course is to help you to improve your language and communication skills of reading, writing, talking and listening. This will undoubtedly help you in your other subjects. More specifically, to achieve success in English, you have to develop and then demonstrate your ability to:

● read, write, talk and listen at National 5 level
● understand, analyse and evaluate texts, including Scottish texts, in literature, language, or media
● create your own written and spoken texts, showing your own language skills.

So, National 5 English is all about language: learning more about it, and showing that you can use it. What level of language should you be aiming for? The key word here is 'detailed'. The language used for National 5 English is described as 'detailed'. Try to keep this word in mind when you are working on your Portfolio, taking part in talk activities, and, of course, when doing your exam.

Reading, writing, talking and listening

Reading

Much of your National 5 English course will concentrate on reading. The key words here are:

Understanding, analysis and evaluation

What do these words mean? These words are not to be taken (or worried about) separately. They are all about responding to something that you have read or watched or listened to. When you respond to a text, can you show that you understand what it is about and what the main ideas are? Can you work out what the writer is trying to do? Is it to persuade you about something? Make you laugh? Make you sad? Can you identify the main techniques that the writer (or talker or filmmaker) has used, and say something about how these techniques help the writer to get meaning across? Can you make some kind of comment about how well this has been done? Can you say what effect all this has had on you? What impact did the story or poem or play or film have on you?

As I said, these things often go together to make up your overall response to something you have read, heard or watched. But try to keep the three elements in your mind:
- Main ideas
- Techniques
- Impact.

When you are reading or watching something try to ask yourself:
- What are the main ideas here? What is the writer trying to say and do?
- Can I see any techniques here?
- How good is it? What is the best bit? Is it making me laugh or cry?

What you should know

The main thing is – you need to have a response. You need to be able to say:
- 'I think the main ideas are …'
- 'I think the writer is trying to …'
- 'I can see that the writer uses this technique because …'

This takes confidence. Often you are not sure. You don't want to say or write an answer because you think you could be wrong. A lot of people who are studying English say, 'It's not easy because there is no right answer.' For others this is one of the best things about studying English – it gives you the freedom to think for yourself and to express your own ideas. But when you are writing about something you have read or watched or listened to, you have to be able back up your ideas with evidence from the text. You have to notice the techniques the writer is using and be able to comment on them.

Thinking skills

Thinking skills are very much part of English National 5. The more confidence you can find in your own ability to think, the better you will do. The exam will expect you to think, not just to recite or repeat learned notes. When you are reading, writing, talking or listening, try to have your own opinions, and learn to value them.

Reading *The Trial*

Say, for example, you were to read *The Trial* by Franz Kafka. (This is a classic with an intriguing, mysterious story line. If you can get into it you will be hooked!)

When you read a book, a magazine or use the internet, have your reading notebook beside you. As you see something interesting, note it down.

> **Hints & tips** ★
>
> It is a really good idea to keep a notebook or logbook so that you can store your ideas and responses to the things you are reading (maybe a novel or pages from the internet). Doing this, you will be gathering evidence for your Analysis and Evaluation unit as well as preparing for the exam.

This could be a summary of the writer's main ideas/themes and/or interesting use of technique.

For practice

Let's try it out with the opening section of *The Trial*. An extract from the opening of the novel is given below. As you read this, have a think about the kind of things you would note down in a reading logbook. Have a go yourself, and then compare what you thought with what I found.

To help you start, have a think about these questions:

- What is this story going to be about?
- What kind of atmosphere is suggested here?
- What are your thoughts about the main character?

The Trial

Someone must have been telling lies about Joseph K., for without having done anything wrong he was arrested one fine morning. His landlady's cook, who always brought him his breakfast at eight o'clock, failed to appear on this occasion. That
5 had never happened before. K. waited for a little while longer, watching from his pillow the old lady opposite, who seemed to be peering at him with a curiosity unusual even for her, but then, feeling both put out and hungry, he rang the bell. At once there was a knock at the door and a man entered whom he had
10 never seen before in the house. He was slim and yet well knit, he wore a closely fitting black suit, which was furnished with all sorts of pleats, pockets, buckles, and buttons, as well as a belt, like a tourist's outfit, and in consequence looked eminently practical, though one could not quite tell what actual purpose it
15 served. 'Who are you?' asked K., half raising himself in bed. But the man ignored the question, as though his appearance needed

⇨

⇨

no explanation, and merely said: 'Did you ring?' 'Anna is to bring me my breakfast,' said K., and then with silent intensity studied the fellow, trying to make out who he could be. The man did not
20 submit to this scrutiny for very long, but turned to the door and opened it slightly so as to report to someone who was evidently standing just behind it: 'He says Anna is to bring him his breakfast.' A short guffaw from the next room came in answer; one could not tell from the sound whether it was produced by
25 several individuals or merely by one. Although the strange man could not have learned anything from it that he did not know already, he now said to K., as if passing on a statement: 'It can't be done.' 'This is news indeed,' cried K., springing out of bed and quickly pulling on his trousers. 'I must see what people these
30 are next door, and how Frau Grubach can account to me for such behaviour.' Yet it occurred to him at once that he should not have said this aloud and that by doing so he had in a way admitted the stranger's right to an interest in his actions; still, that did not seem important to him at the moment. The stranger,
35 however, took his words in some such sense, for he asked: 'Hadn't you better stay here?' 'I shall neither stay here nor let you address me until you have introduced yourself.' 'I meant well enough,' said the stranger, and then of his own accord threw the door open.

Source: Franz Kafka, 'The arrest' from *The Trial*

Answers

Here are a few things that occurred to me as I read the extract. The idea is to note down anything that is interesting or might be important later in the book. Try also to think about the writer's ideas, or themes; often these come across right at the start of a book. You don't need to write down as much as this (you might feel it interrupts your reading), but these are the kind of things you might find. They come in order as they appear on the page.

- First of all, the title *The Trial* – what kind of trial will be involved? Will it be a legal trial, or some kind of test?
- The first sentence: 'Someone must have been telling lies about Joseph K., for without having done anything wrong he was arrested one fine morning.' What an intriguing opening sentence! Who has been telling lies? Why?! What is going to happen to Joseph K. as a result of these lies? Why was he suddenly, unexpectedly arrested? The first sentence sets up the big mystery that the rest of the book will explain. (Note the ironic use of the word 'fine' here. It doesn't look like a 'fine morning' for Joseph K.!)
- Joseph K. – the main character's name. Why just 'K.'? Why no full surname? Does this shortening of his surname mean anything in the book? Is this how some people refer to him? Does it reflect what

⇨

⇨
some people think of him? The main character is mysterious right from the start.

- 'That had never happened before' – the routine of Joseph K. is disturbed. He is unsettled. He is in for an unsettling experience.
- 'the old lady opposite, who seemed to be peering at him with a curiosity unusual even for her' – an atmosphere of people being watched, of paranoia is suggested here.
- 'a man entered whom he had never seen before in the house' – who is this mysterious man? What does he want with K.?
- 'he wore a closely fitting black suit, which was furnished with all sorts of pleats, pockets, buckles, and buttons, as well as a belt, like a tourist's outfit, and in consequence looked eminently practical, though one could not quite tell what actual purpose it served.' – the stranger's strange outfit. Is it some kind of uniform? But not a uniform you would immediately recognise? Some kind of secret organisation, perhaps? Do the belt, buckles, for example, sound threatening? Are the pleats and pockets there to hide things? This description of the stranger's clothes adds to the mystery.
- 'A short guffaw from the next room came in answer; one could not tell from the sound whether it was produced by several individuals or merely by one.' – the stranger has not come alone. There are other people outside. How many? Is the laughter threatening? Does this add to the feeling of paranoia present in the opening of the book?
- 'Yet it occurred to him at once that he should not have said this aloud and that by doing so he had in a way admitted the stranger's right to an interest in his actions' – is Joseph K. starting to feel guilty? Has the trial started already?
- 'threw the door open' – this action of the door being thrown open creates suspense. The reader wants to find out what will happen next.
- Do you feel sympathy for Joseph K.? Do you think he is innocent? Or guilty?
- What are the writer's ideas/themes? Guilt/innocence? Injustice? Paranoia?

Hints & tips ★

This kind of activity is excellent practice for what is required in the Scottish Texts assessment in the exam. Exactly the same skills are needed. Keeping a reading logbook in this way, throughout the year, would be excellent preparation for this part of the exam.

If you fill some pages of a notebook/logbook with ideas that come to you while reading, this will really help when you come to revise literature for the Critical Reading paper. It will also sharpen your mind and improve your reading skills: you will notice more.

It seems to be a fact that people who read do best at school. It's just a fact. (And not only in English – in other subjects, too.)

Professor Stephen Krashen (University of Southern California) said recently:

'The best way to enure pupils develop a strong command of written and spoken English is to encourage wide, self-selected reading.'

Source: *The Guardian*, 30 July 2012

What to read?

Newspapers

Try to read newspapers (in print or online – there are some free ones!). The passages for the Reading for Understanding, Analysis and Evaluation section of the exam tend to be taken from quality newspapers such as these listed below. It is a good idea to be familiar with the kind of writing that comes up. Try to read a good selection.

The Herald
The Scotsman
The Daily Telegraph
The Times
The Financial Times
The Guardian

Novels

Read novels. Plenty of people, books or websites will advise you what to read. Here are just a few suggestions of books that I think you should read:

- *To Kill A Mockingbird* by Harper Lee
- *Animal Farm* by George Orwell (you can read this in one night, it's only 100 pages!)
- *Morning Tide* by Neil Gunn (set in the Highlands of Scotland – I loved it when I was fifteen which was admittedly a long time ago!)
- *Great Expectations* or *A Christmas Carol* by Charles Dickens
- *Tess of the D'Urbervilles* by Thomas Hardy
- *My Family and other Animals* by Gerald Durrell (it's really funny!)
- *Remembrance* by Theresa Breslin
- *Lord of the Flies* by William Golding
- *The Catcher in the Rye* by JD Salinger
- *Murder on the Orient Express* by Agatha Christie
- *The Hound of the Baskervilles* by Arthur Conan Doyle (or any of the Sherlock Holmes novels)
- *The Colour of Magic* by Terry Pratchett
- *The Hobbit* by JRR Tolkein
- *Arthur: the Seeing Stone* by Kevin Crossley-Holland
- *Troy* by Adèle Geras
- *Stop the Train* by Geraldine McCaughrean
- *Kit's Wilderness* by David Almond
- *Fahrenheit 451* by Ray Bradbury (or any of his short stories – great science fiction stuff)
- *2001: A Space Odyssey* by Arthur C Clarke
- *The Time Machine* by HG Wells
- *Junk* by Melvin Burgess
- *Dear Nobody* by Berlie Doherty
- *Fever Pitch* by Nick Hornby
- *Empire of the Sun* by JG Ballard

- *Boys Don't Cry* by Malorie Blackman
- *Crusade* by Elizabeth Laird
- *The Wall* by William Sutcliffe
- *Wuthering Heights* by Emily Brontë

Many of these have all been around for a while now, but they are all great.

A dictionary

If you are serious about doing well in English, you should have a dictionary. I know there are lots of online dictionaries, and they are fine, but there is something valuable about flicking through a printed dictionary: you come across other words as you look! Since I was about fifteen I have tried to look up every word of which I don't the meaning.

Which one to buy? There are lots available – Chambers (particularly good for Scottish words), Oxford and Collins.

Writing

Let's look at making a start at improving your writing skills. Again a notebook is invaluable here, or a file or two on a laptop or other computer. If you become used to writing down your thoughts and feelings as they come to you (as you would in a diary) then you will become skilled in writing about your own experience of literature. In this way, when you are asked to write a personal/reflective essay, you will have material to draw on. If you go further and write about your reactions to events/happenings that feature in the news, then you will be in a great position to write a discursive essay on a topical issue.

Really, you just need to start. Once you have written something you will get into it, and the words will flow. As you write more your mind will bring up words that you have heard and stored away. You probably don't realise that you know them!

Hints & tips

A few writing ideas to help you make a start:

✓ *If you could choose only one colour for all your clothes, what would it be?*
✓ *Describe your house.*
✓ *When have you felt the most nervous? On what occasions in the future do you think you will feel nervous?*
✓ *When you have a problem, whom do you talk to?*
✓ *Do you prefer to be with a large group of friends, by yourself, or with just one or two friends?*
✓ *When were you most happy?*
✓ *What would you change about the way you look?*

Talking and listening

Talking and listening will be done mostly in class: it is very much part of your learning, and your teacher will assess you on these skills. Your teacher will decide when is the right time to carry out the assessment. It may take place over several talking and listening sessions or activities. The assessment can be either group discussion or a presentation. There are four aspects to it. You have to show that you can do all four of these things:

- Employ detailed and relevant ideas and/or information using a structure appropriate to purpose and audience
- Communicate meaning effectively through the selection and use of detailed spoken language
- Use aspects of non-verbal communication
- Demonstrate listening by responding to spoken language

The first bullet point is about the content of your spoken language. Are your ideas detailed? Can you communicate them in a sensible order? Is everything about the content relevant to the topic?

The second bullet point is about the language that you use. Again, is your choice of language sufficiently detailed? Is it clear and accurate enough that people can understand what you are saying?

The third point is concerned with non-verbal communication. This can cause problems for some people, but try not to worry about it. There are many ways to use non-verbal communication: varying your facial expressions; nodding or shaking your head your head; using hand gestures to emphasise a point; shrugging your shoulders, etc. It is not just about eye contact.

The fourth one is where you show your listening skills. If you are taking part in a group discussion, this will involve you making contributions to the discussion which show that you have been listening to the others. For example, you might introduce a point you are making by saying something like 'I agree with what B said, but I would like to say that …' Or, 'I don't agree with that. I think …'

If you are doing a presentation, you will have to answer a couple of questions from the audience at the end.

The main thing to remember for your spoken language assessment is that the ideas you use (in either discussions or individual presentations), and the language that you choose must be *detailed*. This is what your assessor will be looking for: can you communicate detailed ideas, and can your choice of language be called 'detailed'?

Writing – how to get started

'What am I trying to say? What words will express it?'
George Orwell, 'Politics and the English Language'

Creative
Make writing a habit

As I suggested in Chapter 1, at the start of the year, find yourself a notebook. Fill it with sentences, half-sentences, words or ideas that come into your head. Add to it as the year goes on: finish off some of the sentences, add to the words. Use words to describe things you have seen, experiences you have had, events that have excited you or made you angry. You don't need to let anyone else see it. Apart from being a way of engaging with the world and recording your thoughts, this will give you a store of ideas and sentences that can be turned into pieces of writing for your Portfolio. Remember, your Portfolio is worth 30 marks – that is, 30 per cent of your overall award. It is also something with which you can really take your time. You have all year to work on this, to become better at it. For the Portfolio there is no time-limited exam pressure forcing you to work quickly.

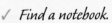

Hints & tips

✓ *Find a notebook.*
✓ *Keep a journal.*
✓ *Keep it going.*

Be positive

Try to approach writing for your Portfolio in a positive way. Your writing is something to be proud of, something you have made yourself. This has come from you – no one else. Try to push yourself. Think to yourself, 'Is this better than I could write a year ago?' Read it over and say, 'That's not bad, actually.' Try not to settle for 'That'll do.' This is why it is better to start early. It is best not to rush things.

Hints & tips

✓ *Look at a piece of your writing from last year.*
✓ *Think to yourself, 'I can do better than that!'*

What to write about?

Well, we are all different. Some of us like to write about things that have happened to us. Perhaps there is an achievement of which you are proud, or something that didn't go as well as you hoped it would, or maybe a tough experience that has been hard for you to work your way through. All of these things have an impact on us, and writing about them can help us make sense of what is going on, or record our thoughts and feelings for the future. Many people, however, do not like to write about things that are personal to them. Given the choice, a piece of short fiction may be more appealing or seem more doable.

Beginning, middle, end

Whatever you decide to write, think beginning, middle and end. You have to bear in mind this basic structure – beginning, middle and end – whether you're writing about something that you have experienced, or are using your imagination to create an experience for fictional characters.

Let's have a look at trying to create a piece of short fiction. What do you need to create?

- Think of two characters.
- Put them into a situation or setting.
- Make something happen (a problem, a conflict).
- Then think of an ending (how is the problem solved or the conflict ended?).

That's it. If you have these things you have a beginning, a middle and an end. You have a story. Keep it simple. It is often a mistake to try to take on too much when writing short fiction, to have a range of characters moving across different settings, with lots of things happening. The problem with this approach is that elements can only be sketched in – there is no depth or development, there is no room to write effectively – because all of the effort goes into telling a complicated plot-line. Also, there is no need to show off all the writing techniques you have learned: try instead to concentrate on using one or two, carefully.

> **Hints & tips** ★
> ✓ Think beginning, middle, end.
> ✓ Keep it simple.

Taking a close look at how it's done

Let's look at a piece of short fiction written by a professional writer. This follows the approach suggested above:

- there are two characters (with a third coming in at the end)
- there is a simple setting
- there is a 'problem' faced by one of the characters, and
- there is an ending.

And that's all. But, from this very simple story there comes a lot of meaning, and an equal amount of emotional power. See what you think. It is by Tove Jansson, and it is called 'Moonlight'. A young girl, Sophia, her grandmother and Sophia's father are spending the summer on a tiny island just off Finland.

Tove Jansson

Moonlight

One time in April there was a full moon, and the sea was covered with ice. Sophia woke up and remembered that they had come back to the island and that she had a bed to herself because her mother was dead. The fire was still burning in the
5 stove, and the flames flickered on the ceiling, where the boots were hung up to dry. She climbed down to the floor, which was very cold, and looked out through the window.

The ice was black, and in the middle of the ice she saw the open stove door and the fire – in fact she saw two stove doors, very
10 close together. In the second window, the two fires were burning underground, and through the third window she saw a double reflection of the whole room, trunks and chests and boxes with gaping lids. They were filled with moss and snow and dry grass, all of them open, with bottoms of coal-black shadow. She
15 saw two children out on the rock, and there was a rowan tree growing right through them. The sky behind them was dark blue.

She lay down in her bed and looked at the fire dancing on the ceiling, and all the time the island seemed to be coming closer and closer to the house. They were sleeping by a meadow near
20 the shore, with patches of snow on the covers, and under them the ice darkened and began to glide. A channel opened very slowly in the floor, and all their luggage floated out in the river of moonlight. All of the suitcases were open and full of darkness and moss, and none of them ever came back.

25 Sophia reached out her hand and pulled her grandmother's plait, very gently. Grandmother woke up instantly.

'Listen,' Sophia whispered. 'I saw two fires in the window. Why are there two fires instead of one?'

Her grandmother thought for a moment and said, 'It's because
30 we have double windows.'

After a while Sophia asked, 'Are you sure the door is closed?'

⇨ 'It's open,' her grandmother said. 'It's always open; you can sleep quite easy.'

   Sophia rolled up in the quilt. She let the whole island float out
35 on the ice and on to the horizon. Just before she fell asleep, her father got up and put more wood in the stove.

Source: 'Moonlight' by Tove Jansson

Creating atmosphere/mood

Now, 'Moonlight' is less than one page of typed script, but it is very, very powerful writing. Look at how effectively the setting and atmosphere are made clear in the very first sentence. We are by the sea and the atmosphere is cold ('covered with ice'), and a little bit mysterious and eerie ('there was a full moon'). Notice how the writer lets us know that Sophia's mother has recently died with the brilliant second sentence:

Sophia woke up and remembered that they had come back to the island and that she had a bed to herself because her mother was dead.

The sentence seems to be all one breath, and is split into three parts by the word 'and'. You can imagine the young girl waking up and thinking, 'I'm awake, where am I?', and then, 'I'm on the island.' You can almost see her patting the bed beside her and wondering why no one is there as she finally remembers that she is sleeping alone because her mother has died. Keeping the news of the mother's death until the end of the sentence is also highly effective because it seems such an understatement, almost an afterthought, and is all the more powerful for that. The mention of death, of course, fits the cold atmosphere that has already been set by the very first sentence.

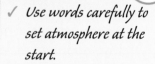

Hints & tips

✓ Use words carefully to set atmosphere at the start.
✓ Position words effectively in your sentences to create impact.

Using colour

The writer then goes on to use a very simple technique that everybody can use: reference to colour. This is very simple to do, but can be very effective. As the girl gets up to look out of the window, Jansson writes, 'The ice was black.' The colour black is associated with death, and also with a dark, cold, frightening mood. It fits perfectly with 'ice'. The sky is described as 'dark blue', another dark colour that fits the mood. When Sophia sees the reflections of the trunks and chests in the window they are described as 'coal-black'.

Simple reference to temperature is used too. Jansson stresses how cold it is outside. This is contrasted with the little bit of warmth inside coming from the 'fire still burning in the stove'. This could suggest the contrast between the sad feelings Sophia experiences from the loss of her mother (her mother has gone away from her, is 'outside of' her), and the comfort she receives from those inside the house – her grandmother and father.

Hints & tips

Colour is a very effective way to suggest feelings or to create a mood.

Using metaphorical language

A very important technique, and one of the main features of creative writing, is metaphor. This is, of course, when a writer compares one thing with another related thing in order to suggest meaning or meanings – to make the meaning stronger, clearer, more powerful, more complex and interesting. In this extract, Jansson uses one main metaphor. It comes in the middle of the extract when Sophia looks out of the window. She sees all the 'trunks and chests and boxes' (in other words their luggage) that have been strangely reflected in the double-glazing as if they are outside. The cases are described as having 'gaping lids' and 'bottoms of coal-black shadow'. As Sophia goes back to bed and begins to fall asleep, in that half-waking mood when you mix your waking thoughts with the beginnings of dreams, she seems to see the suitcases drifting away in the ice:

All of the suitcases were open and full of darkness and moss, and none of them ever came back.

Now, the cases are clearly meant to be metaphor. Using them in this imaginative way, Jansson asks us to think about what the cases could stand for or represent – there is the possibility that the cases could suggest to us the coffin of Sophia's mother, the 'gaping lid' could suggest the recency and rawness of the experience. The gravity and reality of Sophia's loss is brilliantly suggested by the ending of the sentence above: 'none of them ever came back', which suggests that Sophia fully realises that her mother won't be coming back.

Use of conversation/dialogue

Teachers often say that it is difficult to get this right in a piece of creative writing. There is a danger that too much dialogue will take over the storytelling and spoil it. In the extract above, Tove Jansson uses just a little dialogue towards the end. Here, every bit of the dialogue adds to the meaning, nothing is there without a reason.

When Sophia fully wakes up, disturbed by her thoughts in the night, she asks her grandmother, who is sleeping near her,

'Listen,' Sophia whispered. 'I saw two fires in the window. Why are there two fires instead of one?'

Reading this, a clear sense of Sophia's confusion over the illusion caused by the double-glazing, and general upset, comes over in the direct question. Her grandmother's answer gives us a clear sense of *her* personality and attitude to life:

Her grandmother thought for a moment and said, 'It's because we have double windows.'

From this we get the impression that Sophia's grandmother is a practical, down-to-earth person who wants to give her granddaughter a truthful answer about how the world works. Sophia is clearly not reassured, however, as we see from her reply:

After a while Sophia asked, 'Are you sure the door is closed?'

> ### Remember
>
> Metaphor/simile – one thing is compared to another in order to suggest meaning. Similes use the words 'like' or 'as'; metaphors don't. For example:
>
> 'my love is like a red, red rose' – simile
>
> 'my love is a rose' – metaphor.

> ### Hints & tips ★
>
> ✓ Don't overcrowd your writing with lots of different metaphors.
> ✓ When you think of a metaphor, try to develop it to suggest meaning.

To this question I think we would all expect the grandmother to say, 'Of course it's closed, don't worry.' But she doesn't. Instead, she says,

'It's open,' her grandmother said. 'It's always open; you can sleep quite easy.'

This reply confirms what we have already suspected about the grandmother, that she wants to give Sophia a real picture of the world; she doesn't want to give her false expectations. Notice the word 'quite'. It is as if to say, 'You will probably be okay, but I can't guarantee it.'

The point is: all of the dialogue used here is for a purpose. It is to give us further information on the characters, and it adds to the overall meaning of the story. The suggested meaning is, perhaps, that the world is sometimes a confusing and upsetting place, there are people close to us who try to help us, but they cannot protect us from everything.

> **Hints & tips** ⭐
> ✓ Use dialogue sparingly.
> ✓ Use it to give information about characters, or to suggest meaning.

The ending

Sophia rolled up in the quilt. She let the whole island float out on the ice and on to the horizon. Just before she fell asleep, her father got up and put more wood on the stove.

Notice how some of the anxieties, or conflicts, that were set up at the start of the story are answered here. 'Sophia rolled up in the quilt' suggests that Sophia has found some warmth; she has 'let the whole island float out on the ice and on to the horizon.' In a final brilliant touch, Jansson has Sophia's father come in to 'put more wood in the stove'. This seems to suggest that Sophia's father has a role to play in comforting her, too. He provides warmth, but perhaps not through words, more in a practical way.

Clearly, this is just one example of a certain kind of story, and a certain kind of ending. But, in general, an ending should, in some way, round things off. It should refer to conflicts or ideas from earlier in the story, and either take them further or, in some way, settle things.

> **Hints & tips** ⭐
> ✓ An ending should end things.
> ✓ Try to go back to earlier ideas or conflicts in your ending.
> ✓ Try to leave the reader with something to think about.

Personal writing

All of the above is also true of personal writing – you can follow the same shapes and techniques when writing about yourself and your experiences. The difference is that this time you are the character at the centre of the piece of writing. To make this kind of writing work you need to try to bring you-as-a-character to life. You have to explore the experiences you are writing about. You have to think of setting, conflict, and so on, and describe them in as much detail as if you were writing a piece of fiction. You also need to communicate your thoughts and feelings about and reactions to your experiences as fully as you can. I mentioned the importance of thinking skills in the last chapter (see page 2). They are vital here. Try to reflect on the experiences you are writing about. Ask yourself questions like these:

Questions ❓

- What did I learn from this?
- Why was this so important to me?
- Did I, perhaps, change as a result of this?
- Did this affect how I felt about someone or something that was important to me?
- Was I pleased or disappointed by what happened?
- Has time made a difference to how I feel about my experiences?

If you can come up with answers to questions like these, and if you can manage to write about them, then it is likely you will be writing with insight, sensitivity and self-awareness. These words are at the top end of what a marker is looking for in a piece of personal writing.

What to write about

A lot of people find themselves stuck when asked to attempt some personal writing. I hope that keeping a journal (as mentioned on page 9) will produce quite a few possible ideas for further exploration. If you have had experiences in your life that have caused you pain or difficulty, writing about them can help you to feel better about things. Writing about these experiences gives you a chance to think about them fully and to reflect on them. It might work for you. Some people prefer not to go there, however, and choose to write about other things.

Whatever you choose, you have to give the reader a sense that this is a significant experience, or set of experiences, in your life. For example, many people choose to write about sporting achievements. This can produce some really good writing, but be careful. It is better to write a personal/reflective essay on why football is so important to you that mentions a cup final, rather than write a blow-by-blow account of everything that happened in that cup final, even if you can remember every second of it.

Hints & tips ⭐

You can make it clear to the reader/marker that you are trying to reflect on your experiences by using expressions like these:

- ✓ I realise ...
- ✓ Looking back, I now see ...
- ✓ I learned from this that ...
- ✓ I now know ...
- ✓ I could have reacted differently ...
- ✓ Since this happened ...
- ✓ Now that time has passed ...
- ✓ Moving on from this ...

Discursive writing

This is where your thinking skills really come in. To write a successful piece of discursive writing you have to show your thinking. First of all, you have to find a topic that really grabs you, that you care about and that you have strong opinions about. If you have thought of such a topic then you are halfway there. This will come across if you write with conviction about a topic, and your writing will have genuine impact.

- If you feel really strongly about something, then write a persuasive essay in which you try to persuade the reader to take your point of view.
- If you find a topic fascinating, but are not sure which side of the argument you are on, because both sides have valid points, then write an argumentative essay. An argumentative piece is more balanced and two-sided; a persuasive piece has stronger opinions and is more one-sided.

Whatever you choose to write about, you will need to do some research. While it is highly desirable to have opinions about your chosen topic, you will need to have some curiosity, too. A successful piece of discursive writing will show the writer's thoughts and opinions, but these thoughts and opinions will be backed up by evidence. And here is where your study skills and thinking skills really come in. There is a mass of facts, figures and opinions available to everyone online. The challenge is how to use this resource effectively.

When researching online you have to make use of your note-making skills – go for key points, summarise lengthy arguments, select facts and statistics carefully. If you can start to do this well now, you will be laying the foundations for the key skills required at Higher level, and on through Advanced Higher to college and university. In writing a discursive essay you will be practising the same skills that you will need for your Critical Essay in the exam: taking a topic and showing your thinking on it by developing a line of thought.

Activities

Let's take a topic that has caused discussion recently – gun control. What is your reaction to this? Are you for or against more gun control (especially in America)?

Perhaps you have strong views on this subject. If so, you could write a persuasive essay with a clear line, either for or against more gun control. Maybe you are not sure and can see both sides. In this case, you could write an argumentative essay in which you display the arguments from both sides and come to a conclusion that acknowledges both points of view.

Either way, you will need to carry out some research in order to gather evidence.

⇨

Taking as a starting point the shooting at Sandy Hook Elementary School in Connecticut, USA, on 14 December 2012, try to gather an A4 page of evidence on the topic. Remember your note-making skills – main points, summary, key facts and figures.

Did you come up with something like the following box? It is a mixture of facts, statistics and people's opinions.

Example

Discussion topic – should it be illegal to own a gun?

Case study: Sandy Hook Elementary School, Connecticut, USA, 14 December 2012.

Facts: Gunman Adam Lanza, 20, shot and killed his mother, Nancy, before driving to Sandy Hook where he shot and killed twenty children and six adults (including the headteacher, the school psychologist and the Grade 1 teacher), before killing himself. He apparently used three guns: a Glock pistol, a Sig Sauer pistol and a .223 Bushmaster rifle. The guns were legally owned by Nancy Lanza.

Background: This attack was the sixteenth in America in 2012 in which multiple victims were chosen at random.

- On 2 April: seven people were shot dead and ten injured at a shooting in Oikos University, California.
- On 20 July: James Holmes (calling himself the Joker) killed twelve people and injured 58 at a Colorado cinema showing of *The Dark Knight Rises*.
- On 5 August: Wade Michael Page killed six people at a Sikh temple in Wisconsin.

Firearms per 100 people: UK 0.1–10; USA 70–100.

Deaths from firearms injuries in the USA: 30,000 per year. (More than those killed per year in the war in Syria.)

In 2012, James Holmes (mentioned above) was able to buy an AR-15 assault rifle over the counter of a shop. In 90 seconds (before being stopped), he shot 71 people in a Colorado cinema with a weapon capable of firing 60 shots a minute.

In 2011, a Gallup opinion poll in America showed only 26 per cent in favour of gun controls. In 1959 the figure was 60 per cent.

On 14 December 2012 American President Barack Obama gave the strongest hint yet by an American president in favour of gun controls. The only high profile American politician in favour of gun controls is Michael Bloomberg, the New York mayor.

The National Rifle Association (NRA) of America is a very powerful voice against the control of guns. The NRA argues that it is the right of every American to carry a gun in order to defend him/herself.

A history of US mass shootings:

University of Texas, 1 August 1966

After murdering his wife and his mother, Charles Whitman killed fourteen people and wounded 30 others firing from the 28th floor of a university building.

Cleveland Elementary School, 17 January 1989

Patrick Edward Purdy used a semi-automatic weapon to kill five children and wound many others at a school in Stockton, California.

Columbine High School, 20 April 1999

Eric Harris, 18, and Dylan Klebold, 17, murdered twelve students and a teacher at their former high school in Columbine, Colorado. Both killed themselves at the scene.

Virginia Tech, 16 April 2007

Seung-Hui Cho, a student at Virginia Tech, killed 32 people before killing himself. Cho was born in Korea but had been studying English at the university.

Remember

Be careful when selecting evidence. Keep a note of which websites you have used. If you want to use opinions and statements from the writers you have been reading online, remember to use your own words. You cannot copy and paste sentences straight from a source. Markers check this kind of thing, and you could find yourself in quite a lot of trouble for plagiarism. You can't be expected to change everything into your own words (facts and figures, for example), but remember, you have to process your research findings.

Writing a discursive essay

Like any other piece of writing, a discursive essay needs a structure (a beginning, middle and end). In this case, a beginning should be something that grabs the reader's attention (a question, a shocking occurrence, a startling statistic, a provocative statement or quote), and an ending should be a conclusion (balanced, perhaps, or a summing up of the main points; or a quote, a question, a provocative statement or set of figures).

Hints & tips

Think beginning, middle, end.

There are many frameworks or essay plans for pieces of discursive writing. If you prefer the support of a framework then use one, but don't feel that it is compulsory. A discursive essay that contains genuine thinking and real opinions will do just as well, if not better, than an essay that follows a skeleton plan.

A line of thought is very important. Try not to jump around from point to point in your essay. To help you with the flow of your essay and linking your paragraphs, here are some key words:

Key words

- Firstly …
- Secondly …
- Thirdly …
- Therefore …
- Yet …
- On the other hand …
- However …
- Although …
- As a result of this …
- In addition to this …
- Nevertheless …
- Likewise …
- Similarly …
- Consequently …
- In conclusion …
- To sum up …
- Finally …
- On the whole …

Remember

When writing a discursive essay, or any essay at all, remember George Orwell's words quoted at the start of this chapter:

'What am I trying to say? What words will express it?'

Writing is a form of communication. It is a way of putting forward your ideas to someone else (the reader, the marker). Don't think you have to fill your writing with lots of fancy, complicated words. Simple words will do. Aim to be clear. The best way to write impressively is to be clear and fresh in your use of language. As Orwell put it:

'Never use a metaphor, simile … which you are used to seeing in print.'

'Never use a long word where a short word will do.'

'If it is possible to cut a word out, always cut it out.'

George Orwell, 'Politics and the English Language'

Preparing your Portfolio for submission to SQA

As you prepare your Portfolio for submission to SQA for marking, there are a few important things to remember:

- Your teacher can talk to you about your ideas for writing, but don't expect your teacher to give you a specific plan. The rules do not allow for this.
- You are entitled to advice on one draft of each piece of writing. Make use of this. When your teacher gives you suggestions, try to act on them and make improvements to your writing.
- Be very careful with plagiarism. Make sure that you acknowledge all sources you have used at the end of your writing. If you are using a quote from research you have done, make sure you put quotation marks round the words you have taken. Otherwise, be very careful to use your own words.
- Read your Portfolio pieces carefully before submitting them. Accurate proof reading can make a big difference to your writing. Again, don't rely on your teacher for this. SQA guidelines don't let your teacher go through every piece, correcting all errors in spelling and punctuation.
- Remember that there are word limits: 1,000 words for each piece.

Exam section 1: Reading for Understanding, Analysis and Evaluation

Building your skills

In this chapter we shall look at a skill that is, of course, at the heart of any work in English – reading. The activities here will help you to build your skills at reading closely and carefully, and will help you to prepare for the Reading for Understanding, Analysis and Evaluation section of the exam.

WAGES

Carer, banker, footballer: who really deserves the big bucks?

Who's worth more? The carer who drops in on your elderly parent three times a day? The footballer whose skills you admire so much? The head of one of our prestigious universities? Or the cleaner who freshens up your hotel room?

5   The simplest way to answer this question lies in how much they get paid. Footballers top the league: Lionel Messi has become the world's first footballer to clear £1m a week. The vice-chancellor of the University of Bath, the country's top paid university chief, commands a salary of more than £450,000.

10   At the other end of the scale, the Spanish women cleaning the hotel rooms of British holidaymakers typically earn less than £13,000 a year.

The care sector is one of the worst culprits when it comes to non-compliance with national minimum wage legislation: the
15   Resolution Foundation has estimated frontline care workers collectively miss out on over £100m a year due to non-payment of the legal minimum.

However, it seems obscene that a university vice-chancellor might be worth more than 30 times someone doing emotionally
20   and physically difficult care work. As soon as we start to probe the philosophical basis of our grounds for assessing what we deserve, questions about the financial worth of someone's work become much more complex.

What are we looking to reward? Effort or natural talent or some
25   mix of the two? Why is it fair that someone born with the raw talent to excel at sport could go on to make so much more than someone who doesn't? Isn't this just brute luck?   ⇨

This is perhaps why it's rare in the popular debate to see high pay justified purely with reference to what we deserve. Instead,
30   its defenders tend to hide behind the market: we need to pay people extortionately to attract the top talent.

The truth is that high pay is rarely driven by unique talent or market forces. Instead it's a reflection of the value society puts on different kinds of work.

35   We place little value on work, largely carried out by women, such as caring: bizarrely, we continue to reserve more respect for the financiers who crashed the global economy. Until we face up to this, astronomical pay will be here to stay.

Source: *The Observer,* 16 July 2017 (adapted)

What are the writer's main ideas?

Let's look at the way the writer has put this piece together: the basic structure. From this we'll see what the article contains; the main ideas will emerge as we go:

- A set of questions, asking about the worth of different jobs in our society.
- Figures stating what people doing these jobs get paid.
- Comment on wide differences in pay.
- More questions, asking how it is that rewards are worked out/decided on.
- Conclusions drawn as to what society really values.

We can say then, that the main ideas here are:

- There are huge differences in pay in different areas of our society.
- These differences say something about the way we value people and their jobs.
- This does not seem fair.

How does the writer use language?

On a quick reading of the article, are there any language techniques that you notice straight away?

Perhaps the most obvious thing is the writer's use of questions. There are five in the first paragraph alone, and they appear again in the middle of the short article. The use of so many questions probably tells us something about the writer's purpose in this article: the writer wants us to question the hugely different levels of pay across our society, and then ask ourselves: is this fair? If you look closely at some of the questions, you can discover more about the writer's attitude to the issue. Take these questions, from the middle of the article:

'Why is it fair that someone born with the raw talent to excel at sport could go on to make so much more than someone who doesn't? Isn't this just brute luck?'

Here you can clearly see that the writer does not think this is fair. The questions help us to realise that the writer is being critical of society's methods of payment and reward.

If you look closely at the writer's choice of words, you will see that these too show us that the writer is critical of pay inequality. For example, take the word 'bizarrely' (from the final paragraph). This word suggests that society's attitudes are very strange, in fact, almost unbelievable. Consider another expression from later in the paragraph: 'astronomical pay'. The word 'astronomical' is powerful here. It suggests that the level of pay is so high that it is really out of this world – it is 'astronomical', so high it is in outer space.

So, you can see how the writer has used both sentence structure and word choice to make clear criticism of the way that pay works in our society.

Remember

Tone – the writer's attitude towards the particular subject he/she is writing about (think tone of voice, e.g. sympathetic, aggressive, and so on).

Example

Now, let's look at a piece of writing with a very different attitude, a very different purpose:

In praise of … Paddington Bear

Fifty years ago a stowaway bear from darkest Peru arrived in London clutching a battered suitcase. Welcomed into the home of Mr and Mrs Brown, and renamed after the station where he was found, Paddington stepped into the lives of generations
5   of children. With his red bush hat and blue duffel coat – and, of course, with a marmalade sandwich in hand – he remains instantly recognisable. To mark the half-century his creator, Michael Bond, has written *Paddington Here and Now*. In his first novel in 29 years, Paddington faces his most threatening
10   adventure: he has a run-in with police and is interrogated over his residency status. It is easy for us to forget that Paddington is an immigrant – a refugee at that – so long has he been around; he seems as British as they come. In creating him Bond had in mind the child evacuees who fled wartime London with
15   labels tied around their necks. But Paddington's journey is also representative of all those from abroad who have made for London during his long years in the city. And can there be a better model than Mr and Mrs Brown for the open and welcoming Britain to which we should aspire? Or than Paddington himself, ⇨

20 with his polite manner and sunny optimism, for the kind of temper citizens should have? Few are quite so fond of marmalade nowadays, and the endearing bear represents a post-war milieu that has passed. But Britain must always make room for those, like Paddington, who 'try so hard to get things right'.

Source: *The Guardian*, 2 June 2008

Activity

Try these two questions on 'In praise of … Paddington Bear':

1 How does the writer use the example of Paddington Bear to make a serious point about Britain today?
2 Look at the last four lines of the passage ('Few … right'). What tone is adopted by the writer in these lines, and how does he achieve it?

Answer

1 How does the writer use the example of Paddington Bear to make a serious point about Britain today?

Through the use of an example from a work of fiction, the writer has shown that in the past British people have welcomed immigrants (often refugees) not only into the country, but also into their affections.

The social values represented in the fictional character of Paddington Bear (good manners, a positive outlook on life) are ones that should be fostered in British society today.

Answer

2 Look at the last four lines of the passage ('Few … right'). What tone is adopted by the writer in these lines, and how does he achieve it?

There are a few possible answers here. In reading assessments, it is often not the case that there is just one answer. There may be several possible answers – all of which are acceptable.

Answers

● The writer adopts a tone of nostalgia (affection for things past). He does this by including favourable references to years gone by – 'Few are quite so fond of marmalade nowadays' and 'represents a post-war milieu that has passed'.
● An affectionate tone also comes across. The word 'endearing' in the expression 'the endearing bear' suggests fondness and affection.
● Finally, there is a tone of positivity or encouragement in 'Britain must always make room for those …' Here the expression of instruction, 'must always', suggests encouragement.

In 'In praise of … Paddington Bear', the writer has created tones through his careful selection of words. Frequent exam questions concern a writer's use of language. In this type of question you have to have the confidence to look for specific ways in which a writer has used language to make his meaning clear, or to emphasise or highlight certain aspects of it.

One of the ways to tackle this common question is to have a quick scan of the passage (or the section of the passage you have been asked to deal with), identifying any features of the language that stick out. Try it with 'In praise of … Paddington Bear' (this is a short passage, so it shouldn't be too hard to spot a few things). Scan the passage quickly, then give yourself one minute to make a quick list of any language features that you can spot.

When you try to scan a passage looking for language features, often the things that stand out first are punctuation marks or markers to do with sentence structure. Maybe these were the first things that you noticed here. Towards the end of the passage there are two questions. Here the writer uses questions to ask the reader to think seriously about the kind of society he or she wants to live in. He challenges us, through the use of questions, to take up the kind of values that Paddington represents (welcoming others, having good manners, being optimistic).

You may well have noticed the dashes in the first half of the passage. The dashes contain groups of words that are not essential to the sentences in which they appear (this is called parenthesis). If you try to read each sentence without the words in dashes you will find that they make complete sense. In this passage, however, there are two examples of parenthesis being used; each example is slightly different. Look at the first example:

With his red bush hat and blue duffel coat – and, of course, with a marmalade sandwich in hand – he remains instantly recognisable.

Here the writer uses parenthesis to offer additional information (information that is not necessary to the sentence). The extra information here is the fact that Paddington enjoys marmalade sandwiches. Why has the writer done this? He has done this to emphasise (or add to) his point that Paddington is instantly recognisable. Now have a look at the second example:

It is easy for us to forget that Paddington is an immigrant – a refugee at that – so long has he been around; he seems as British as they come.

In the second example the use of parenthesis is slightly different. Here the writer makes an aside (he adds in an extra direct comment to the reader). He is saying to the reader that not only is Paddington an immigrant, he is technically a refugee. Here the writer uses parenthesis to clarify his point about Paddington's status in British society. He is suggesting that we should accept immigrants and refugees into our society in the same way that we have accepted Paddington Bear.

Next on your list may well have been the use of a colon (two dots, :) in this sentence:

In his first novel in 29 years, Paddington faces his most threatening adventure: he has a run-in with police and is interrogated over his residency status.

What follows the colon is an explanation of Paddington's 'most threatening adventure'. This helps to make clear that, in this article, the writer is concerned with issues around immigration and British society's attitude towards immigrants.

However, most examples that you find of a writer's use of language will be to do with word choice. The words used by a writer give you the clearest indication of what they are really concerned with, what they want you to think about, and what they want to achieve. Going into the exam, you must try to find the confidence to identify key words that the writer uses and, most importantly, you must be able to make a comment on the meaning of these words and their importance in what the writer is trying to say (his/her argument).

At this level, most people can find key words without a problem. The difficulty (and often the loss of marks) comes from a hesitation over the comment. The comment is often under-developed or just repeats the words of the question. You have to try to think it through – what do these words really mean? Why does the writer choose them? Often the words used by a writer mean something quite specific in that particular example. Take, for example, the use of the word 'temper' in this passage. It comes in this section:

And can there be a better model than Mr and Mrs Brown for the open and welcoming Britain to which we should aspire? Or than Paddington himself, with his polite manner and sunny optimism, for the kind of temper more citizens should have?

Now, when you think of the word 'temper', my guess is that you will think right away of temper tantrums, of someone who is easily angered. But that doesn't sound quite right here, does it? If you look at the words around 'temper' they are all to do with calm, positive things – 'polite manner', 'sunny optimism'. In this case 'temper' means a frame of mind or mood. The words around it provide clues – 'sunny optimism' and 'polite manner' are examples of states of mind or mood.

Working towards the real thing

Now for a longer passage. This one is roughly the size of the passage you will have to deal with in the examination. The passage is about the British Olympic champion athlete Jessica Ennis (now Jessica Ennis-Hill).

What drives Jessica Ennis?

Three months ago Jessica Ennis won Olympic gold, confirming her status as both the friendly face of the Games and a ruthless winner.

Jessica Ennis-Hill

After trying and failing to find Jessica Ennis in the English Institute of Sport in Sheffield, a female athlete helps me track
5　her down. 'There she is,' she says. Which is just as well as I'm not entirely convinced I'd have recognised the slight figure in tracksuit bottoms and a hooded top.

I'm 5ft 10in, Ennis is just 5ft 5in, and with her muscles covered up and her six-pack under wraps, she seems teeny tiny, all
10　skinny shoulders and narrow hips. If I hadn't seen her in action with my own eyes, and I didn't know she was the Olympic heptathlon champion, a sport which essentially involves being world class in seven different disciplines, I honestly would have said that I could have had her in an arm-wrestling match.

15　One of her trainers, Mick Thompson, recalls seeing her at an athletics open day which her parents had taken her to age 10, and says that, 'she stood out a mile … she was probably one of the most talented youngsters I've ever seen.' We've become used to seeing these amazing physical freaks, the Michael Phelpses and
20　Serena Williamses of the world, but Jessica Ennis just seems to be a perfect distillation of pure athleticism and absolute willpower.

In her about-to-be-published autobiography, *Unbelievable*, she recounts how before her first event in the Olympics, her mum sent her 'usual' text message: 'Don't let those big girls push
25　you around.' They didn't, of course. She didn't let them. Over the course of two days, and seven events, Ennis beat off the big girls and took gold in the Olympic stadium in a moment of high emotion in the middle of what came to be known as Super Saturday.

30　Two and a half months on, and, she says, 'It still hasn't worn off.' Has she had post-Olympic blues? 'People ask me that,' she says. 'They say, isn't it an anti-climax? But it's been the best experience ever. And I'm still so busy trying to fit everything in. But it's still amazing. Every time my dad comes around, he's like:
35　"You're an Olympic champion!" Everyone is still on a high.'

But, she says, it's 'weird' when she goes out. 'You can hear people talking about you. And sometimes they see me and just go: "Jessica Ennis!" like that in my face and then don't know what to say. But everyone is so sweet. They all just want to tell
40　me their story. "I was there!" or "I watched you and you made me cry." That's one I've heard a few times.'

Jessica Ennis wasn't just carrying her own hopes and dreams into the Olympic stadium, she had the wonderful but terrible psychic burden of carrying all of the rest of ours, too, because
45　spontaneously and without actually asking her, the media, sponsors and Olympic organisers collectively decided that she was the face of the Games.　⇨

⇨ 'I don't really know how that happened,' she says. 'One journalist asked me, "Did you apply for that?" Like it'd been
50 advertised or something. But, of course, I didn't. I really don't know why. It just sort of happened.'

But everyone else knows exactly why. Her Olympic performance in the heptathlon was nothing short of spectacular. But it was her post-Olympic performance, that lovely genuine smile she
55 has and the absolute heartfelt joy she showed in winning that cemented her reputation as one of the nicest people in sport.

But the pressure! In retrospect, and having read her autobiography, I'm amazed she didn't simply crack up. It's no coincidence, it seems to me, that in the ladies' loo at the
60 Institute of Sport there's a poster with a tense-looking woman on it. 'Feeling under pressure?' it asks. 'Ring the Samaritans.'

In Sheffield alone, she would pass five massive banner posters of herself on her way to training. She recalls how she once went out for a bag of chips and thought better of it when she
65 saw herself blown up 20 times life-size above the chip shop, the acme of physical perfection, and 'drove on to the supermarket instead'. The first thing that athletes arriving into Heathrow saw was a field-sized portrait of her face next to the runway. And arriving in Stratford, one athlete tweeted that it was like landing
70 'in a Jessica Ennis theme park'.

Success has mostly been strange-good for Ennis, rather than strange-strange. She's almost universally loved. The nation's newest sweetheart. It's not difficult to see why she became the poster girl for our British twenty-first-century Olympics:
75 hard-working but good-humoured, humble but determined, the smiling multicultural embodiment of how we'd like to see ourselves as a nation. And when, despite the pressure, she came good, on Super Saturday, it's not a huge stretch to see that somehow, we did, too.

Source: *The Observer*, 4 November 2012

Questions

1 Look at the first paragraph and then explain, using your own words where possible, why the writer had difficulty in finding Jessica Ennis.
2 In paragraph 3, Ennis is described as the 'perfect distillation of pure athleticism and absolute willpower.' What do you think this means?
3 Look again at paragraph 5 and explain how the writer uses contrasting word choice to help you to understand the expression 'post-Olympic blues'.
4 Look at paragraphs 7–11 and explain fully, in your own words, how the writer develops the idea that 'Jessica Ennis wasn't just carrying her own hopes and dreams into the Olympic stadium.'
5 Show how two examples of the writer's use of language in the final paragraph help to create a positive image of Jessica Ennis in the reader's mind.

Answer

1 Look at the first paragraph and then explain, using your own words where possible, why the writer had difficulty in finding Jessica Ennis.

Reading from the start of paragraph 1, the writer makes it clear that she has needed help to 'track her down'. Spotting this in the paragraph, you will realise that you are close to finding the answer. Just after this comes:

Which is just as well as I'm not sure I would have recognised the slight figure in tracksuit bottoms and a hooded top.

There is something here that suggests that the writer has had difficulty in finding Jessica Ennis – 'I'm not sure I would have recognised' – and the reason why – she is a 'slight figure in tracksuit bottoms and a hooded top.' Having found this, your next challenge is to attempt to change this into your own words. You might go for 'identify' for recognise, and then you might be a little stuck over 'slight figure'. Well, you don't need to use complicated vocabulary in your answer, something like 'small person' would do fine. Then you would have to look at 'tracksuit bottoms and a hooded top'. For that you could simply summarise: 'in normal training clothes'. Your whole answer might go something like this:

The writer does not find Jessica Ennis herself – someone has to point her out. The writer doesn't identify right away the ordinary looking smallish person wearing normal training clothes.

Answer

2 In paragraph 3, Ennis is described as the 'perfect distillation of pure athleticism and absolute willpower.' What do you think this means?

The key to answering this question is the word 'distillation'. It is not an everyday word, but you might recognise another word within it that is associated with something else – 'distil', as in to distil whisky. Another meaning of 'distil' is to 'extract (or take out or remove) the essential meaning of'. This is what it means here.

If you look at the context, again it will help you with this question:

We've become used to seeing these amazing physical freaks, the Michael Phelpses and Serena Williamses of the world, but Jessica Ennis just seems to be a perfect distillation of pure athleticism and absolute willpower.

We already know that Jessica Ennis is a 'slight figure', not at all like the 'amazing physical freaks' mentioned here. But she shares something with the 'amazing physical freaks', in that she has 'pure athleticism and absolute willpower'. The difference is that she has these things distilled down. She has essential/concentrated amounts of fitness, skill and determination. Once again, the words around the key expression (the context) help you to come to the meaning. But you have to look – you have to think about it.

Answer

3 Look again at paragraph 5 and explain how the writer uses contrasting word choice to help you to understand the expression 'post-Olympic blues'.

Let's start with 'post-Olympic blues'. 'Post' means after. 'Blues' (as in to sing the blues) means sadness. Look for contrasting words or expressions. Positive/happy/excitement-type words for the success Jessica had at the Olympics, and contrasting words that you would associate with sadness.

Positive, happy, etc.

- 'best experience ever'
- 'on a high'
- 'Olympic champion'.

Opposite feelings (sadness, etc.)

- 'worn off'
- 'anti-climax'.

Answer

4 Look at paragraphs 7–11 and explain fully, in your own words, how the writer develops the idea that 'Jessica Ennis wasn't just carrying her own hopes and dreams into the Olympic stadium.'

To answer a question about a writer developing an idea, look for other words/expressions that are ideologically similar to the ones specified. In this question we are looking for words/expressions that suggest that Jessica Ennis was carrying the hopes and dreams of other people as well as her own. Remember that you are directed where to look – paragraphs 7 to 11.

Answers

What can we find?

- The 'face of the Games' – she came to represent all that the Games stood for.
- Reference to 'Ring the Samaritans' – this shows the pressure she was under due to expectations.
- The 'five massive posters of herself' – public constantly reminded of her.
- The 'field-sized portrait of her face' – representing the huge scale of pressure/expectations.
- 'Jessica Ennis theme park' – her image/likeness is everywhere – the expectations are high.

As you can see, a quote plus comment approach is a good way to answer a question like this.

Answer

5 Show how two examples of the writer's use of language in the final paragraph help to create a positive image of Jessica Ennis in the reader's mind.

Question 5 is interesting because it asks you to look at the writer's use of language. It doesn't specify what to look for. It doesn't identify word choice, or sentence structure, or imagery. You have to make that decision yourself. It is a good idea to indicate the type of language use you are going for at the beginning of each part of your answer. Let's see what we can find.

Word choice

- She's 'universally loved' – the word 'universally' suggests everyone and everywhere. There is a high regard for Jessica Ennis everywhere and by everyone.
- The 'nation's newest sweetheart' – a 'sweetheart' is someone who is loved. There are positive feelings towards her. Notice the writer also uses alliteration to draw attention to the phrase. That's something else you could say.

Sentence structure

- The writer uses short simple statements to stress the positives:

  She's almost universally loved.

  The nation's newest sweetheart.

- Notice that the second sentence contains no verb – it is a minor sentence. This is another way that a writer uses sentence structure to draw attention to certain ideas.
- In the sentence below, notice that the writer uses a colon (:) to introduce a list of the positive qualities that Jessica Ennis possesses.

  It's not difficult to see why she became the poster girl for our British twenty-first-century Olympics: hard-working but good-humoured, humble but determined, the smiling multicultural embodiment of how we'd like to see ourselves as a nation.

Remember

Alliteration – words in an expression that start with the same sound. Used to emphasise key words.

You are now ready to try the real thing. Three full Reading for Understanding, Analysis and Evaluation papers follow in the next chapter. Again, help is given with finding the answers.

Before you move on, try this quick exercise. It is a completely different type of writing and subject matter.

Orphans

They were not all literally orphans. They were often cast out, or they ran out themselves, from families too big or too small to support them. In the prevailing conditions of extreme poverty, children might be carried along by the family only through the
5 nursing stage, and then they would be expected to provide their own sustenance. Frequently enough, there was not room for them so they willy-nilly had to find other accommodation, often at an age when children in our time are not yet allowed to cross the street. Historians have noted that childhood was not
10 recognised as a particular state until recent times, and point to paintings of the sixteenth or seventeenth centuries, in which children are depicted as miniature adults. In New York this idea was still operative among large sections of the poor in the nineteenth century. Children in the nineteenth-century slums
15 were not only accorded all the responsibilities and attendant hardships of adulthood without the advantages of strength and experience; they were expected to cope with the single item of particular status conferred upon them: invisibility.

Until the reformers of the 1890s began making public the plight
20 of New York's poor children in sweatshops and on the street, such children simply went unnoticed. This had its advantages and disadvantages. It made theft, for example, more convenient. It also means that today we can get only the most rudimentary and indeterminate idea of the numbers involved. In 1849 it
25 was estimated that there were 40,000 homeless children in Manhattan; in the 1860s, between 10,000 and 30,000; in 1871 the estimate was 28,610. Children on their own were of necessity members of the criminal and mendicant classes; if they were employed, they were de facto enslaved. They slept on the docks,
30 in cellars and basements, in alleys and doorways. Sleeping outdoors was already known then as 'carrying the banner'. A 'country visitor' quoted by the reformer and missionary Charles Loring Brace in 1876 wrote that 'two little newsboys slept one winter in the iron tube of the bridge at Harlem; two others made
35 their bed in a burned-out safe in Wall Street. Sometimes they ensconced themselves in the cabin of a ferry-boat, and thus spent the night. Old boilers, barges, steps, and, above all, steam-gratings, were their favourite beds.' They burrowed into the empty and derelict spaces, not that there were many in a city
40 where adults fought for sheltered hallways and cellar corners. Being small and beneath notice gave them the mobility as well as the status of rats.

Source: Luc Sante, *Low Life* (adapted)

Questions ?

1 What does 'cast out' in line 1 mean?
2 Can you put 'In the prevailing conditions of extreme poverty, children might be carried along by the family only through the nursing stage' into your own words?
3 Looking at the whole of the first paragraph, what were the main differences between childhood, and attitudes towards childhood, then and now?
4 Which words from the first sentence of the second paragraph link well with the end of the first paragraph?
5 In your own words, what were the 'advantages and disadvantages' of children being 'unnoticed' by the adult world?
6 Many children then had the 'status of rats'. In which ways does this sum up the main ideas of the passage?

Answer

1 What does 'cast out' in line 1 mean?
'Cast out' – thrown out

Answer

2 Can you put 'In the prevailing conditions of extreme poverty, children might be carried along by the family only through the nursing stage' into your own words?
At that time people were very poor, and children were only given close attention in the very early stages of their lives.

Answer

3 Looking at the whole of the first paragraph, what were the main differences between childhood, and attitudes towards childhood, then and now?
Main differences – children then had to be much more independent than they have to be now; they were treated like adults but without the development and resources that adults had.

Answer

4 Which words from the first sentence of the second paragraph link well with the end of the first paragraph?
Linking words – 'such children were simply unnoticed' from the first sentence of paragraph 2 goes well with 'invisibility' from the end of paragraph 1 (a link is established).

Answer

5 In your own words, what were the 'advantages and disadvantages' of children being 'unnoticed' by the adult world?

● Advantages – stealing was easy.

● Disadvantages – children were very often homeless and when they could find work, they were, more often than not, exploited.

Answer

6 Many children then had the 'status of rats'. In which ways does this sum up the main ideas of the passage?

'Status of rats' – this sums up the main ideas of the passage because children then often had to 'run out' or run away in the same way that rats do. They had to find shelter, find food, and live unseen the same way that rats do. They were also, in some ways, unloved, as are rats.

Chapter 4
Exam practice

How can you revise for, or prepare for, the Reading for Understanding, Analysis and Evaluation part of the exam?

The best way to do this is to familiarise yourself with, and practise, the kind of questions that will come up in the exam. In this chapter there are three sets of passages and questions which mirror the exam format. When you think you are ready, have a try at these, comparing your answers with the ones provided. I have tried to explain how you come to find the answers, so, if you are stuck on a question, have a look at the answers and you should be able to move on.

In this article by D T Max, the writer examines a possible place for robots in our schools.

A Whole New Ball Game
The rolling robot that teaches kids to code (to programme) computers

At a school in Denver, Colorado, the old America is giving way to the new. A stuffed grizzly bear that once stood at the entrance has been banished to a dusky back hall-way, and many of the students are the children of tech workers. On a recent
5   Monday morning, a science teacher shouted from the front of the classroom, 'Grab your iPads and your Spheros!' When her command didn't work, she clapped twice, and this code was successful: her two dozen students clapped back, roughly in unison, and began getting up from their desks. The students
10 grabbed their Spheros – milky white orbs about the size of large oranges – and hurried to the school's former library, now known as the Digital Commons.

You tap a Sphero twice to turn it on, and it flashes three colours in quick succession; once it has established a link to your iPad
15 or your smart-phone, it strobes like a fortune-teller's crystal ball and is ready to move. A Sphero is chiefly a toy. You download an app, and, by pressing and swiping and swirling your finger on your smart-phone or tablet screen, you can command the ball to travel a zippy five or so miles an hour on land. A Sphero can
20 make hairpin turns, and thanks to its gyroscope, it is aware of your location; with one gesture, you can order it to roll back to you. It will vibrate softly, like a purring cat, and you can code it to do a lot of fanciful things: dance, perform playful flips, find its way around the things it bumps into, and blink if it falls over an
25 edge. Because it looks like an ordinary ball, it outperforms your expectations.   ⇨

⇨

Spheros aren't just fun; they are also an excellent teaching tool. Students have begun to use them to learn everything from geometry to genetics. They can code them, too, to take a

30 first step into computer programming. For the inventors who came up with the Sphero, it was a fortuitous moment to create such a crossover product. The STEM movement – the effort to incorporate science, technology, engineering, and mathematics into the classroom – was gaining in popularity. Educators avidly

35 debated how to help kids make the transition from the analog world of early childhood to the digital world of adults. Many teachers foresaw a crisis: only sixteen per cent of school pupils contemplate a career in STEM fields, even though the number of STEM jobs is increasing rapidly. Sphero and similar toys like

40 Lego Mindstorms – simple robots that you build and then code – have come to be seen as stops on the road to the well-paid position of programmer.

Not everyone who is interested in children's education is impressed, however. For them, the benefit of moving young

45 children from tactile experience to the world of screens is unclear. After all, Steve Jobs wouldn't allow his children to use iPads, steering them instead toward books and conversation. The inventor of the Sphero, by contrast, told me that if he had children he would definitely encourage them to be online.

50 'Everything I know I learned from the Internet,' he said.

Putting young children in front of screens will likely make them better coders, but what will go unlearned during these hours? Education is not merely job training. And some studies suggest that the more children interact with devices the harder time

55 they have interacting with one another. Yet electronic gadgets are tempting for teachers, especially a gadget like Sphero, whose surface has two cute blue dots and an upswept blue line, suggesting a tiny face.

The teacher's goal that day was to harness the class's ongoing

60 study of the environment to promote some basic programming skills. Hope and achievement sometimes coincided. Three students suggested that they could save a koala from hunters by attaching a Sphero to its back. They created a maze to simulate a path out of the forest. After twenty twists and turns, the

65 Sphero, weaving and bobbing nimbly, found its way to safety.

Later, I visited another school where the Spheros are locked up in the computer lab, like children in a fairy tale. But a few students had been given permission to try to get their Spheros to go thirty feet down a hallway, loop under a hurdle that had

70 been borrowed from the gym, then return to the starting point. There was a cheat: they could just drive them with their fingers, using the preinstalled software. Sometimes the children did this, sometimes they coded. They flitted in and out of the two without particular concern. Was it playful coding or code-filled play? One

75 student, Megan, smoothly pulled down commands and got her

Sphero to roll, execute a nice circlet, and come back. She also programmed it to light up in different colours to make it 'pretty'.

80 The makers of Sphero want to start building robots that forge an emotional attachment with their owners. Sphero encourages users to name their orbs, and the children I saw playing with them clearly regarded them as more than machines. Last month, I watched two young students play with Dash and Dot, a pair of robots that have anthropomorphic features. After programming them, one girl set them face to face. 'I'm going to make them 85 kiss,' she said.

At Sphero's headquarters a veteran gaming programmer is creating backstories for future products. The first one will be a robotic incarnation of a well-known comic-book superhero. The makers promise, 'You'll be able to bring him into your home and 90 have a conversation with him where he engages and starts to learn about you.'

For Sphero, this is just a beginning; it wants its robots to not only learn your needs but communicate their own. They want their next brainchild to become the friend you call on to listen to your 95 problems or help with your homework. 'It's got to become part of the family,' a spokesman said. 'And by becoming part of the family, it has to know its environment and know the people in the family and change its behavior based on who it's interacting with. We're not trying to make a robotic pet. We're making a pet 100 robot, really. They'll come with a brain and a past.' When I told him I'd like such a robot as long as I could turn it off, he smiled a gentle smile. If their robot was successful, he answered, I'd feel bad if I did.

Source: Adapted from an article by D T Max, in *The New Yorker*.

Exam-style questions

1 Look at lines 1–12. By referring to two examples, explain how the writer's use of language makes it clear that 'the old America is giving way to the new'. (4 marks)

2 Look at lines 13–26, and then identify, using your own words as far as possible, five key features of the Sphero. (5 marks)

3 By referring to the sentence 'Spheros aren't just fun; they are also an excellent teaching tool' (line 27), explain how it helps to provide a link between the writer's ideas at this point in the passage. (2 marks)

4 Look at lines 27–42 and, using your own words as far as possible, identify two points the writer makes to explain why it was the right time for the invention of Sphero. (2 marks)

5 Look at lines 43–58 and explain, in your own words as far as possible, two advantages and two disadvantages of new technology like Sphero. (4 marks)

6 Explain fully why the simile 'like children in a fairy tale' (line 67) is effective here. (2 marks)

⇨

7   Look at lines 67–77 ('But … pretty') and explain how one example of word choice and one example of sentence structure help to make it clear that the children are learning and/or playing. (4 marks)

8   Look at lines 78–91, and identify, in your own words as far as possible, five points the writer makes about robots becoming like humans. (5 marks)

9   Select any expression from lines 92–104, and explain how it contributes to the passage's effective conclusion. (2 marks)

Answer

1   Look at lines 1–12. By referring to two examples, explain how the writer's use of language makes it clear that 'the old America is giving way to the new'. (4 marks)

This is an example of an analysis question. Here you have to show that you can analyse the ways in which a writer has used language to make a point clear. You have to find two examples of the writer's use of language and you then provide a comment for each of them. The comments have to be relevant to the point identified in the question – ways in which 'the old America is giving way to the new.' A good way to start would be to find one example of language which points to the 'old', and one example which emphasises the 'new'. In this type of question you are allowed to choose which language feature(s) you are going to comment on.

The model for your answer here is: quote plus comment, x2 = four marks. You will be given one mark for a relevant quote (or reference), and one mark for a suitable comment. A good way to set it out is to write down your quote (or reference) followed by your comment, as below.

Answers

- Word choice: Old
  - 'stuffed grizzly bear' – a dead, preserved animal, or animal skin is something we wouldn't tend to have in schools nowadays. It would be more likely in past times.
  - 'once' – this word suggests that time has passed, or things have changed due to time passing.
  - 'banished' – suggests something being left behind, or sent away (in this case relating to time).
  - 'dusky back hall-way' – suggests a place forgotten about in time.
  - 'former' – suggests something that is not used anymore.
- Word choice: New
  - '(the children of) tech workers' – the word 'tech' suggests modern or up-to-date.
  - 'iPads … Spheros' – these words relate to modern inventions.
  - '(milky white) orbs' – suggests futuristic objects.
  - 'Digital Commons' – a new, modern version of a library.

Marks

Two references plus two comments would mean four marks.

Answer

2   Look at lines 13–26, and then identify, using your own words as far as possible, five (key) features of the Sphero. (5 marks)

In this type of question, you are asked to show how well you have understood the main points that a writer makes in a specified section of the text. The question will always tell you which part of the passage to look at for your answer. Here it is lines 13–26 (the second paragraph). The question will let you know how many points you should look for. Here it is five. The main thing to remember is that, you have to use your own words in your answer. If you just lift the words from the passage you will be given no marks. But notice the wording of the question: 'using your own words as far as possible'. It will be almost impossible to find your own words in some cases (e.g. 'phone', 'iPad', etc.), and the marker will be tolerant here.

You will see that there are plenty of options for answers below.

Answers

- Sphero is operated by touch control – 'You tap a Sphero twice to turn it on'.
- It lights up to indicate that it is working – 'it flashes three colours in quick succession'.
- It works with other technology – 'established a link to your iPad or your smart-phone'.
- You can play with it – 'A Sphero is chiefly a toy'.
- You operate it from your phone/tablet, etc. – 'You download an app, and by pressing, swiping and swirling your finger on your smart-phone or tablet screen'.
- It moves quite fast – 'a zippy five or so miles an hour on land'.
- It can go round corners – 'can make hairpin turns'.
- It knows where you are – 'it is aware of your location'.
- It is easy to operate – 'with one gesture'.
- You can make it do what you want – 'you can order it …'/ 'you can code it …'.
- It can do various moves – 'dance, perform playful flips, find its way around the things …'.
- It will indicate if it is in danger – 'blink if it falls over an edge'.
- It can do amazing things – 'it outperforms your expectations'.

Marks

Any five points for five marks.

Answer

3   By referring to the sentence 'Spheros aren't just fun; they are also an excellent teaching tool' (line 27), explain how it helps to provide a link between the writer's ideas at this point in the passage. (2 marks)

This is a question on structure. It is asking you to show your understanding of the ways in which the writer links ideas together. To answer this type of question, you should try to pick out a part of the sentence and comment on how it relates or links to an idea which comes before or after it in the passage.

Answers

- 'Spheros aren't just fun' looks back to 'dance' or 'playful flips' etc.
- 'an excellent teaching tool' looks forward to 'learn everything' or 'first step into computer programming'.

Marks

Either of the above points would be given two marks. Part of each answer would be given one mark (e.g. 'Spheros aren't just fun' looks back – one mark).

Answer

4   Look at lines 27–42 and, using your own words as far as possible, identify two points the writer makes to explain why it was the right time for the invention of Sphero. (2 marks)

This is an understanding question (like number 2 above). The task here is to read lines 32–42 again and pick out two points the writer makes about the time being right for Sphero to come along. Once you think you have found the points made, the next and very important challenge is to put these ideas into your own words. (Notice, again, that there are words like 'science', 'engineering', etc. that you will not be expected to find your own words for.

Answers

- Science and technology subjects were growing or becoming more prominent in schools – 'The STEM movement – the effort to incorporate science, technology, engineering, and mathematics into the classroom – was gaining in popularity.'
- Teachers wanted to help students get ready for the technology-based world they would be growing up into – 'Educators avidly debated how to help kids make the transition from the analog world of early childhood to the digital world of adults.'
- More and more jobs were to be found in science and engineering – 'Many teachers foresaw a crisis: only sixteen per cent of school pupils contemplate a career in STEM fields, even though the number of STEM jobs is increasing rapidly.'

$\Rightarrow$

⇨
- Sphero fitted in with other 'toys' like Lego – 'Sphero and similar toys like Lego Mindstorms'.
- Sphero could help young people to get good jobs in computing – 'seen as stops on the road to the well-paid position of programmer'.

Marks

Any two from the above points. One mark for each.

Answer

5 Look at lines 43–58 and explain, in your own words as far as possible, two advantages and two disadvantages of new technology like Sphero. (4 marks)

In your answer to this question, you have to make four points: two advantages of new technology suggested by the writer, and two disadvantages. The only way to achieve full marks is to cover both advantages and disadvantages. One again, you have to identify the points from the section identified, and then write them down in your own words. Bullet points can be a good way of doing this.

Answers

- Advantages
  - The internet can help people find out about many things – "Everything I know I learned from the Internet".
  - Time spent on technology will help children to learn how to programme – 'Putting young children in front of screens will likely make them better coders.'
  - Technology is an attractive teaching tool – 'electronic gadgets are tempting for teachers'.
  - Some technology can seem almost human – 'suggesting a tiny face'.
- Disadvantages
  - Technology is not real/we can't properly be in touch with it – 'the benefit of moving young children from tactile experience to the world of screens is unclear'.
  - One of the creators of technology (Steve Jobs) encourages his children to talk and read instead.
  - Too much technology will mean missing out on other education – 'what will go unlearned during these hours?'.
  - Learning should not just be about employment – 'Education is not merely job training.'
  - Too much technology can cause social/friendship issues for young people – 'the harder time they have interacting with one another'.

Marks

Any two points from the advantages and disadvantages sections above would be given four marks.

Answer

6 Explain fully why the simile 'like children in a fairy tale' (line 67) is effective here. (2 marks)

A simile is, of course, a comparison, where the writer compares one thing to another (using the words 'like' or 'as') in a way which adds to meaning. Teachers often teach the analysis of similes (or metaphors) by using a pattern: just as … so …To use a famous example: in the poem of the same name, Robert Burns uses the simile 'My love is like a red, red, rose.' We can analyse this by using the 'just as … so … pattern' in this way:

'Just as a rose is beautiful, associated with summer, attractive, so my love too is beautiful, attractive, associated with happy times, etc.' In this way your analysis covers the literal description of the rose with the metaphorical suggestions about the person the poet is writing about. There are no set ways to answer a question like this, but the approach described here might help.

Answers

- Just as, in fairy tales, children are often imprisoned, locked away, hidden, so the Spheros in this school seem mostly to be kept out of sight/out of reach.
- To take another approach, you could comment on similarities between the two elements of the simile: both could be seen to be young; both could be seen to be in some way 'trapped' (locked in the computer lab, kept in school); both could be seen to be held back from what they want to do (Spheros are locked up/switched off, the children want to play instead of being in school!).

Marks

Two marks for either the first approach or two areas of similarities identified using the second approach.

Answer

7 Look at lines 67–77 and explain how one example of word choice and one example of sentence structure help to make it clear that the children are learning and/or playing. (4 marks)

This is an analysis question, but notice that this question does not allow you to select your own language feature – it asks for word choice and sentence structure. This means that you have to deal with one example of each feature to achieve the full four marks. As for question 1, you need a reference plus a comment for each. Note that the question gives you the option to concentrate on learning or playing, or both.

⇨

⇒

Answers

- Word choice
    - 'loop'/'hurdle' – suggest athletics or sport (play)
    - 'starting point' – suggests part of a game (play)
    - 'cheat' – one kind of strategy in a game (play)
    - 'software'/'coded'– aspects of computing (learning)
    - 'commands' – suggests following instructions (learning)
    - 'roll'/'circlet' – suggest movements associated with a game (play)
    - 'light up (in different colours)' – suggests fun/enjoyment (game)
- Sentence structure
    - 'But …' – suggests a change of direction in writer's line of thought (to Spheros being used for learning and play).
    - Long sentence ('But … starting point') – reflects different stages of the Sphero challenge.
    - Use of colon ('There was a cheat:') – to introduce explanation of the 'cheat'.
    - Use of question ('Was it playful coding or code-filled play?') – helps to emphasise the writer's point about playing and learning being closely related.

Marks

Two references (one from sentence structure and one from word choice) plus two appropriate analytical comments would give four marks.

Answer

8 Look at lines 78–91, and identify, in your own words as far as possible, five points the writer makes about robots becoming like humans. (5 marks)

This is another understanding type question. This time you have to identify five points the writer is making about robots becoming like humans. As well as using your own words, the particular challenge here is in finding and isolating five points in quite a small amount of text (two smallish paragraphs).

Answers

- Robots will be able to become the friends of humans/care about them – 'forge an emotional attachment with their owners'.
- Robots will be personalised – 'name their orbs'.
- People will treat robots as they would people – 'regarded them as more than machines'.
- Robots will look like humans – 'have anthropomorphic features'.
- Robots will seem to have feelings – "I'm going to make them kiss'".
- Robots will have personal histories – 'creating backstories for future products'.

⇒

- You will be able to talk to robots – "have a conversation with him'".
- Robots will seem to take an interest in humans – "he engages and starts to learn about you'".

Marks

Any five points from the list above. One mark each.

Answer

9 Select any expression from lines 92–104, and explain how it contributes to the passage's effective conclusion. (2 marks)

This, like number 3, is a question on structure, and is the other common type. For this question, you should aim to select and write down a reference from lines 92–104 and then try to relate it to an earlier reference, or one of the main overall ideas of the passage.

Answers

- 'this is just a beginning' relates to 'giving way to the new' at the start of the passage.
- 'learn your needs' repeats idea of 'starts to learn about you'.
- 'the friend you call on'/'part of the family' repeats idea of 'forge an emotional attachment with their owners'.
- 'robotic pet'/'pet robot' repeats earlier idea of 'name their orbs' etc.
- 'They'll come with a brain and a past' repeats earlier idea of 'creating backstories'.
- 'I'd feel bad if I did' repeats earlier idea of 'tiny face'/'emotional attachment'/'anthropomorphic features' etc.
- OR any of the above references could be related to a main idea of the passage.

Marks

Reference plus a linked reference or explanation from elsewhere will be given two marks.

This article by Emine Saner introduces the modern magician Dynamo.

Dynamo, the magician who walks on water

Dynamo

This is a story about poverty, bullies and nineteen prize-winning golden retrievers. But most of all, about magic. Not the rabbit-from-a-hat, creepy holiday-camp entertainer kind of magic, but the sort of trickery that feels so fresh it turns bullish hip-hop
5 artists and football stars into giggling children. Mobile phones miraculously appear in beer bottles. The magician can vanish and reappear on the other side of a glass window. His shows are shocking – he swallows necklaces and pulls them out of his stomach – and delightful. Last year he walked on the River
10 Thames near the Houses of Parliament. Dynamo is a slight figure, dressed casually in a red jacket and trainers, looking like he'd just got off the bus.

That's why it works, I think – an ordinary kid who can do extraordinary things. A magician whose fans are very familiar
15 with the idea of a young wizard with a difficult childhood, whose discovery of his magic powers changed his life.

His first television series brought in an average of 1.7 million viewers – this, on a non-Freeview channel called Watch, which would consider anything over 100,000 a success. What is the
20 appeal? He leans back and thinks. He doesn't look all that ordinary when you study him – he has weirdly blue eyes, and although small and narrow, he looks nimble and fleeting, as if he could fly off at any second. 'In this day and age, you walk down the street and you've got everything shoved in your face.
25 We're in a consumer market where we're constantly force-fed, we consume what's given to us. But most people like what they don't understand. They like mystery.' When he walked on water, 'I didn't tell anybody I was going to do it, I didn't advertise it. It was about that moment, and anybody who
30 happened to be there got to witness a spectacle that will never happen again. It's always about keeping that sense of wonder. I get to create little moments of astonishment.'

But times aren't so great for other television magicians with both the BBC and ITV cancelling traditional magic shows. 'I
35 believe that part of it was that the style of the shows was still that clichéd magician,' he says. 'Shiny-floor shows in general, studio-based shows, have kind of been done to the hilt. There's so much competition out there, and I think they weren't doing anything that was different enough to keep people interested.
40 But the magic on the shows was amazing – people like Penn and Teller are geniuses. I hope I'm as successful as them in years to come.' The mainstream channels must be casting a greedy eye over him. He sinks back into his sofa. 'I guess so, but I'm happy with Watch at the moment. Everyone has knocked us back over
45 the years.'

⇨

⇨ So what's next? Does he feel he has to keep going bigger and better?

The new series features one illusion where he walks down the side of the *LA Times* building. 'I don't really like to put a scale
50 on what I do. I treat walking on the Thames with the same approach as I treat a pack of cards. It's more about how amazing the magic is. I like doing magic with nothing, like just my hands.' He bends his little finger as if it were clay – the same trick he once showed a horrified Prince Charles. He takes the pack of
55 cards on the table in front of us, shuffles them, hands as fast as dragonflies, and makes one of the cards disappear in his hand, then reappear. I feel myself do a cartoonish, wide-eyed gasp. He smiles. He never gets tired of people's reactions, he says.

Dynamo grew up moving around some of Bradford's most
60 deprived housing estates. He has three half-siblings, but they are much younger, so he spent much of his childhood as an only child. Or a 'lonely child' as he puts it. He moved in with his grandparents (actually, his great-grandparents) when he was sixteen.

65 His great-grandfather Ken was a Second World War veteran who had learned tricks in the navy. He died earlier this year, but lived long enough to see his great-grandson well on his way to becoming a magic superstar. 'The first thing he ever showed me was how to take away the bullies' strength,' he says. The trick
70 he learned – he still uses it today, once to baffle the heavyweight boxer David Haye – makes him impossible to physically pick up.

Rumours spread around the school that he had superpowers. 'At the beginning, people thought I was weird, but slowly it got to the point where people wanted to see me do things. Magic,'
75 he says, 'gave me the power to bring people to me. It gave me an edge, something to make me unique. The only reason I stood out before was being the smallest kid in school. This made me different, but in a way that was positive.'

He decided on a career in magic, and thought going to live in
80 Las Vegas would be the best way to do it. His grandmother lives in America and spent her time travelling to dog shows. 'She has nineteen award-winning golden retrievers,' he says. 'She was doing a tour of America, and invited me to go with her. She was going to places I wanted to go, like Vegas and New Orleans,
85 quite magical. I saw this as a learning experience.'

A born blagger, he got past doormen and backstage security guards and persuaded numerous celebrities, such as Chris Martin, Ian Brown and Snoop Dog, to appear on his self-made DVD, *Underground Magic*, which came out in 2005. 'I made the
90 DVD, put it on the website and with no advertising sold 8,000 copies in a month.'

⇨

⇒ It would have been easy, he says, with his celebrity contacts –
Lewis Hamilton is a friend, but there are plenty of others,
including Richard Branson, Will Smith, Tinie Tempah, Rio

95 Ferdinand and Wayne Rooney – 'to come back with series two
all glitzy and glam, but what we've done is allow people who
have supported it from the beginning to pick up where we left
off and come along for the journey. You see it going from me
still being relatively unknown to shutting down Westfield when I

100 went shopping [he tweeted he would be there and thousands of
people turned up]. I had to have eight security guards to get me
out. You see the transition from being a normal guy to…'

He pauses. I can feel eyes on us through the window behind
me as time runs out and the people around him start to worry

105 about the next stop on his schedule. 'It's very weird. I don't
think I'll ever fully feel this is normal. It's crazy the way people
have taken to me and my show. One thing the first series gave
me, the success of it, was the confidence that people like me for
who I am. For the first time in years, I feel accepted.'

Source: *The Guardian*, 7 July 2012 (adapted)

Exam-style questions

1 Look at lines 1–16.
   Explain how three examples of the writer's word choice make it clear that
   Dynamo's magic is new and different. (6 marks)
2 Look at paragraph 3 (lines 17–32) and explain in your own words four
   ways in which Dynamo is not, in fact, ordinary. (4 marks)
3 Explain the part played by lines 46–47 in the structure of the writer's
   argument. (2 marks)
4 Look at lines 52–58 and show how two examples of the writer's use of
   language help to make clear the impressive nature of Dynamo's magic.
   (4 marks)
5 Look at lines 59–78 and identify four main points the writer makes about
   Dynamo's childhood in England. (4 marks)
6 Look at lines 79–102.
   Using your own words a far as possible, identify four ways in which
   Dynamo's life has turned around since going to America. (4 marks)
7 The sentence 'He pauses.' (line 103) signals a change of tone in the writer's
   telling of Dynamo's story.
   Explain what this change of tone is and go on to explain how the writer
   uses word choice to make this clear. (3 marks)
8 By summarising the main points the writer makes, identify three things
   you have learned about the magician Dynamo from this article. (3 marks)

Answer

1 Look at lines 1–16. Explain how three examples of the writer's word choice make it clear that Dynamo's magic is new and different. (6 marks)

In this analysis-type question, you have to find three examples of the writer's word choice that make it clear that Dynamo's magic is fresh, and different to what magic was like before he came along. There are words here which describe dynamo's magic directly, and there are words which refer to what magic was like in the old days. You can use either in your answer.

Answers

- Dynamo's new approach
  - 'fresh' suggests brand new, exciting, etc.
  - 'miraculously' suggests something so incredible it can't be explained.
  - 'shocking' suggests disturbingly new.
- The old-fashioned approach
  - 'rabbit-from-a-hat' suggests the oldest trick of them all.
  - 'creepy' – suggests watching the old magicians made you feel uncomfortable.
  - 'holiday-camp entertainer' – suggests out of date/past times.

Marks

Three references plus three comments would give six marks.

Answer

2 Look at paragraph 3 (lines 17–32) and explain in your own words ways in which Dynamo is not, in fact, ordinary. (4 marks)

Again this is a case of finding relevant information, description, ideas from a chunk of text and changing them into your own words. If you look at the identified paragraph you will see that in lines 20–21 the writer notes, 'He doesn't look all that ordinary when you study him.' What follows is an explanation of how Dynamo is not ordinary. This is where you will find the answer to the question.

Answers

- His eyes are a strange colour/he looks at you strangely/piercingly – 'he has weirdly blue eyes'.
- He is very quick/very light/like a spirit – 'he looks nimble and fleeting, as if he could fly off at any second'.
- He has incredible talent/skill – 'When he walked on water'.
- He does not boast about his skills/achievements – 'I didn't tell anybody I was going to do it, I didn't advertise it'.

Marks

One mark for each of the above points.

Answer

3 Explain the part played by lines 46–47 in the structure of the writer's argument. (2 marks)

You need to be able to show some understanding of how a writer puts together a piece of writing – of how there is a beginning, middle and end, how things are linked, and so on.

Answer

You will notice that lines 46–47 contain two questions ('So what's next? Does he feel he has to keep going bigger and better?'). The writer has described what Dynamo has achieved so far; he is going to go on to look at what could be next for him. This line links what the writer has just been dealing with (what Dynamo has achieved) to what he is moving on to (what is next for Dynamo).

Marks

One mark for identifying that the writer asks a question.
One mark for identifying that he goes on to answer the question.

Answer

4 Look at lines 52–58 and show how two examples of the writer's use of language help to make clear the impressive nature of Dynamo's magic. (4 marks)

This type of question asks you to analyse the writer's use of language. You are not told what to analyse – you have to make that decision for yourself. The usual things to look for are: word choice, imagery/comparisons, sentence structure, punctuation, tone.

Word choice

● 'horrified' – this word implies a very strong reaction to Dynamo's impressive magic.
● '(wide-eyed) gasp' – as above.

Imagery/comparisons

● 'He bends his little finger as if it were clay' – comparing his finger to the soft material of clay shows that he can manipulate it in an impressive way.
● 'hands as fast as dragonflies' – his movements are incredibly quick.

Sentence structure

● 'He smiles.' – this very short sentence puts emphasis on Dynamo's reaction to his own magic – he knows it is impressive.

Marks

Two examples of use of language plus two comments would mean four marks.

Answer

5 Look at lines 59–78 and then sum up in your own words the main points about Dynamo's childhood in England. (4 marks)
This question tests your summary skills. Can you go to this section and pick out four points about Dynamo's childhood? Having found them, you have to change the writer's points into your own words.

Answers

- Dynamo started life in Bradford (remember there are some words you will not be able to change).
- He lived in a poor area – 'most deprived housing estates'.
- He has (three) half-brothers/sisters.
- He was isolated when young – 'only child'/'lonely child'.
- He lived with his grandparents/great-grandparents when he was an older teenager.
- His great-grandfather knew some magic – 'had learned tricks in the navy'.
- His great-grandfather taught him his first trick.
- Magic singled him out at school/made him different.
- He was small in size while at school.

Marks

One mark for each of the above (up to four marks).

Answer

6 Look at lines 79–102.
Using your own words as far as possible, identify four ways in which Dynamo's life has turned around since going to America. (4 marks)
For this question, you need to find four ways in which Dynamo's life changed when he went to America. The challenge here is to identify and separate out four points because they all seem quite similar.

Answers

- A new world was opening up for Dynamo – 'She was going to places I wanted to go, like Vegas and New Orleans'.
- It was like a dream to go there – 'quite magical'.
- He worked with famous people – 'persuaded numerous celebrities … to appear on his self-made DVD'.
- He has famous mates – 'Lewis Hamilton is a friend'.
- He is now recognised by the public when he goes out – 'shutting down Westfield when I went shopping'.

Marks

Any four of the above points for four marks.

Answer

7   The sentence 'He pauses.' (line 103) signals a change of tone in the writer's telling of Dynamo's story.
    Explain what this change of tone is and go on to explain how the writer uses word choice to make this clear. (3 marks)

The mood, or tone, of the writing changes in the last paragraph. Having just talked about all the success he has achieved, Dynamo becomes thoughtful and moves on to acknowledge the strangeness, the oddness of his sudden fame.

In questions asking you to comment on word choice, try to pinpoint the significant words. Don't just go for a general comment.

Answer

- The mood becomes thoughtful/reflective.

Word choice

- '(It's very) weird' – the word 'weird' sums up the strangeness of Dynamo's sudden fame.
- 'I don't think I'll ever fully feel this is normal.' – the word 'ever' emphasises the fact that Dynamo thinks fame is a strange experience.
- 'It's crazy' – the word 'crazy' points to the strangeness of fame.
- 'For the first time in years, I feel accepted.' – the word 'accepted' shows Dynamo reflecting/thinking about his fame and what it has meant for him.

Marks

One mark for an identification of mood/tone.
One mark for an example of word choice.
One mark for an appropriate comment.
Three marks in total.

Answer

8   By summarising the main points the writer makes, identify three things you have learned about the magician Dynamo from this article. (3 marks)

Three marks are on offer here, so you should aim to make three points in your answer. Try to think of this as a summary question and take points from the beginning, middle and end of the passage.

Answers

Main points:

- Dynamo is not a traditional type of magician.
- He seems to be ordinary, but can do incredible things.
- He wants to adopt a new approach to magic.
- He did not have a privileged childhood.

- He went to America and this changed his life.
- He has worked with celebrities/has celebrity friends.
- He is now very famous.
- Magic has changed his life/how he feels about himself.

Marks

Any three points. One mark for each point.

In this article, Barbara McMahon explores the phenomenon of young children who are addicted to gadgets.

The iPaddy

Ask any parent what can tip their toddler into a fit of the screaming furies and right up there with being asked to eat broccoli or put on a warm coat will be the taking-away-the-iPad moment. As the gadget is prised from sticky fingers, there will
5 be wails and tears from tiny children who seem to have become tech addicts. So common is this kind of toddler tantrum that it even has its own name, the iPaddy.

Young children – even infants – are spending more of their time with digital technology, and parents are both fascinated and
10 worried by this development. Log on to YouTube and there are dozens of videos posted by proud parents showing cute kids, some still in nappies, jabbing and swiping screens like geeks in Silicon Valley.

But while parents hope that all this digital time is giving their
15 offspring a kick-start on numeracy or learning French, they are also wondering what it is doing to young brains. Seeing a child in a trance in front of a screen, head down and oblivious to anything else going on around them, or having a mini meltdown when the device is taken away, is making parents feel uneasy.

20 Hanna Rosin, writing about the subject in *The Atlantic* magazine, calls it the neurosis of our age. 'Technological competence and sophistication have not, for parents, translated into comfort ⇨

and ease,' she writes. 'They have merely created yet another sphere that parents feel they have to navigate in exactly the right
25   way... Parents end up treating tablets like precision surgical instruments, gadgets that might perform miracles for their child's IQ and help him win some nifty robotics competition – but only if they are used just so. Otherwise, their child could end up one of those pale, sad creatures who can't maintain eye contact and
30   have an avatar for a girlfriend.'

Research suggests that children of preschool age are spending increasing time with their faces a few inches away from screens instead of entertaining themselves with traditional toys or reading books. More than half of children aged up to eight are
35   estimated to have access to an interactive device such as an iPhone, an iPad or some other tablet – in addition to television. Young children can spend up to three hours a day on screen media and even infants under a year old can consume up to two hours a day.

40   While studies suggest that television holds little educational value for under-3s, very young children may be able to learn more from interactive gadgets. This follows the 'video deficit' theory that shows that under-3s learn better from real-life interaction than from watching a video.

45   In one of many studies that prove the theory, children aged 30 to 36 months were better at remembering where puppets were hiding in a room if they had to press a button when they saw the puppets, compared with toddlers who only saw a video of the puppet show.

50   This means that compared with the passive activity of watching TV, interactive devices are likely to be more stimulating, positive and educational for toddlers.

'Having a person on screen talk to a child and respond to them seems to help them learn,' Dr Heather Kirkorian, of
55   the University of Wisconsin-Madison, says. 'So touch-screen technology might actually afford some educational value.'

A recent study found that three-year-olds taking a vocabulary test improved their score by 17 per cent after using an educational app based on word games.

60   Researchers are, however, concerned about the length of time young children spend with digital media, and say screen time should never replace human interaction.

'The greatest touch screen in the world of a child is an adult face,' points out Lisa Guerney, author of *Screen Time*, a book that
65   looks at how electronic media affect children. 'Social interaction is the crucible of learning for young children – they need a person that they can have a back-and-forth conversation with, who can respond to their questions and direct their play,' she adds.

⇨
She describes a video on YouTube that has been viewed by more
70 than half a million people, which shows a boy aged about one
year sitting rapt in front of an iPad, watching a cartoon cat called
Talking Tom. The boy says some nonsensical words and the cat
repeats the chatter back to him. The child does not know, of
course, that he is not communicating with a living creature.

75 'When I see that video it's charming and it makes me laugh, but
it also shows how hardwired we are to want to talk to something
that talks back to us.'

Guernsey says that parents should think about the three Cs:
content, context, and the child's individual needs. Games don't
80 all have to be educational – something parents put forward to
assuage their discomfort about their children using interactive
devices – but they do need to be high quality.

She points out that we don't force children to read textbooks
at bedtime so it's all right to let them have some playtime
85 based round an app. The best apps, she says, don't dictate how
children play but let them use their imaginations.

She understands parents who worry that a tidal wave of media
is washing over their children. 'We're losing sight of the fact that
it's not as if – puff! – childhood has changed overnight.' After
90 all, children still play with dolls and trains and do make-believe,
which is backed by the fact that bouncy balls, Scrabble and a
butterfly garden kit feature in Amazon UK's list of bestselling toys.

It's important to remember that children obsessed with gadgets
eventually balance it out with other activities. Hanna Rosin
95 says she gave her four-year-old carte blanche to use an iPad.
Eventually he lost interest and now picks it up only occasionally.
And what of the trance-like state that children adopt when
staring at iPads or other devices? The experts say parents
shouldn't worry too much – they are simply concentrating like
100 they would if they were playing snap.

Source: *The Times*, 26 March 2013 (slightly adapted)

Exam-style questions

1 Explain how two examples of the writer's use of language in paragraph 1
(lines 1–7) help make clear what she means by the 'iPaddy'. (4 marks)
2 Look at lines 8–19. Explain how two examples of the writer's use of
language make it clear that parents are 'both fascinated and worried' that
their children are spending 'more of their time with digital technology.'
(4 marks)
3 In line 21 the writer calls technology 'the neurosis of our age' for parents.
How does the writer develop this idea of technology being a worry for
parents in lines 21–30? Use your own words where possible. You should
make four key points in your answer. (4 marks)
⇨

⇨

4 Look at lines 40–59 and then identify in your own words four main points the writer is making in these lines. (4 marks)

5 Look at lines 63–77 and explain using your own words as far as possible how the writer develops the idea that 'screen time should never replace human interaction.' You should make four key points. (4 marks)

6 How effective do you find the words 'tidal wave' (line 87) as an image to illustrate parents' fear of the media? (2 marks)

7 Using your own words as far as possible, explain the positive conclusion drawn by the writer in the final paragraph (lines 93–100). You should make three key points. (3 marks)

8 Identify five main points the writer makes in this article about children's use of gadgets. Use your own words as far as possible. (5 marks)

Answer

1 Explain how two examples of the writer's use of language in paragraph 1 (lines 1–7) help make clear what she means by the 'iPaddy'. (4 marks)

A 'paddy' is a fit of temper – interestingly, it is a term derived from 'paddywhack', meaning an 'Irishman given to brawling' (Concise Oxford Dictionary)!

There are plenty of examples of word choice in this paragraph that give a clear idea of this kind of behaviour. You must quote two, and comment on them both (separately).

Answers

- 'screaming furies' (line 2) – this suggests hysterical behaviour (the Furies were three Greek goddesses associated with punishment).
- 'eat broccoli'/'put on a winter coat' (lines 2–3) – these are things associated with tantrums.
- 'prised (from sticky fingers)' – the word 'prised' suggests the parent having to use some force, and this again suggests tantrum-like behaviour.
- 'wails' (line 5), 'tears' (line 5) – words associated with tantrums.
- 'toddler tantrum' (line 6) – the alliteration here draws attention to the word/idea of a tantrum.

Marks

Two examples of the writer's use of language plus two comments would mean four marks.

Answer

2 Look at lines 8–19. Explain how two examples of the writer's use of language make it clear that parents are 'both fascinated and worried' that their children are spending 'more of their time with digital technology.' (4 marks)

⇨

⇨
In your answer to this question you have to deal with two things –
how parents are 'fascinated', and how they are also 'worried'. The marks
will be split over the two sides to your answer. You will be given marks
for your answer on 'fascinated', and you will be given marks for your
answer on 'worried'. (Notice, if you want to draw a marker's attention
to a word in your answer it is a good idea to underline it.)

'Fascinated'

- 'dozens of videos (on YouTube)' (line 11) – the word 'dozens'
  suggests that parents are keen to show off their children's
  technological habits.
- 'proud parents' (line 11) – the word 'proud' suggests that parents
  are pleased with their children's behaviour and want to show off
  about it.
- '(like) geeks in Silicon Valley' (lines 12–13) – parents consider their
  children to be as tech literate as originators/developers of computer
  technology.

'Worried'

- '(Seeing a child) in a trance' (line 16) – the alarming hypnotic effects
  of screen watching.
- '(head down and) oblivious to anything else going on around him'
  (lines 17–18) – concerning lack of awareness of surroundings.
- 'mini meltdown (when the device is taken away)' (lines 18–19)
  – concerning over-reaction/breakdown when technology is
  removed.

Marks

One mark for reference, one mark for comment for each half of the
question. Four marks in total.

Answer

3 In line 21 the writer calls technology 'the neurosis of our age' for
  parents.
  How does the writer develop this idea of technology being a worry
  for parents in lines 21–30? Use your own words where possible. You
  should make four key points in your answer. (4 marks)

Two skills are needed here. Firstly, can you identify/extract the
main points from this section? Secondly, can you change the writer's
words into your own? It is a good idea to bullet point your answer,
as below.

Answers

- Children's familiarity/skill with gadgets has not meant happiness for
  parents.

⇨

⇨
- Parents are anxious about how to approach children's use of gadgets.
- Parents feel pressure to make sure children are using gadgets for the 'right' (that is, educational) reasons.
- Parents feel if technology is not used properly there can be disastrous consequences for children.

Marks

One mark for each point. Four marks in total.

Answer

4 Look at lines 40–59 and then identify in your own words four main points the writer is making in these lines. (4 marks)

As with the previous question, you could bullet point your answer, as below.

Answers

- Young children do not learn much from watching TV.
- Children learn more from live, two-way conversations.
- But, young children do learn from interactive technology.
- Technology can, therefore be beneficial to learning.

Marks

Any four points. One mark for each point.

Answer

5 Look at lines 63–77 and explain using your own words as far as possible how the writer develops the idea that 'screen time should never replace human interaction.' You should make four key points. (4 marks)

When a question asks you to make 'reference to the text', this means that you should quote from the relevant section and then comment on the quote.

Answers

- 'The greatest touch screen in the world of a child is an adult face' – this stresses the importance of face-to-face (human) communication.
- '(children) need a person they can have back-and-forth conversation with' – communication should be two-way.
- 'who can respond to their questions and direct their play' – human interaction provides a response and offers the possibility of guidance.
- 'how hardwired we are to want to talk to something that talks back to us' – we have an inbuilt need for conversation.   ⇨

Marks

Four clear points would be given four marks.

Answer

6 How effective do you find the words 'tidal wave' (line 87) as an image to illustrate parents' fear of the media? (2 marks)

In questions on imagery, the fuller your explanation the more marks you will be given. Remember, for an image, or a metaphor, a writer is comparing one thing to another in order to explain something, or to suggest meaning or feeling. In a full explanation you should try to make clear what the writer is comparing and why. In this example the image is taken from the sentence, 'She understands parents who worry that a tidal wave of media is washing over their children.' She is comparing the media to which children are exposed to a tidal wave. Try to think of how these two things are similar, and relate it to parents being worried.

Answer

The media is compared with a tidal wave. A tidal wave is huge, covers everything in its path and is destructive. The media is also huge in scale, and could be said to 'drown' children in their messages. This causes parents concern.

Marks

Two clear points of analysis would be given two marks.

> ### Remember
>
> There is a helpful formula that might help you to answer this type of question: 'just as ... and so ...', e.g. 'Just as a tidal wave is powerful, huge and destructive, so the media are also unstoppably powerful and destructive. This causes parents to worry.'

Answer

7 Using your own words as far as possible, explain the positive conclusion drawn by the writer in the final paragraph (lines 93–100). You should make three key points. (3 marks)

Answers

- Children don't stick to one toy/interest.
- They move on frequently from one toy to another.
- Children are not dangerously hypnotised by gadgets.
- When they seem to be hypnotised they are only paying (careful) attention.

⇨

Marks

Full explanation using your own words and covering the points above would be given three marks.

Clear explanation using your own words and covering some of the points above would be given two marks.

Weak explanation or not successfully using your own words would be given one mark.

Answer

8 Identify five main points the writer makes in this article about children's use of gadgets. Use your own words as far as possible. (5 marks)

This is a summary question asking you to isolate four of the writer's main points. Try to look at the passage in sections, and to sum up each section. Try not to include examples or what is called supporting detail. Just go for the main points.

Answers

- Children's use of gadgets/technology is growing fast.
- It is difficult to persuade them to put the gadgets down.
- Parents have mixed feelings about this and they are concerned.
- Interactive gadgets might be better educationally for children than watching TV/DVDs.
- Face-to-face conversations with a child have most impact on a child's learning.
- Some aspects of what gadgets offer can be positive/beneficial.
- Parents should not worry unnecessarily about the use of gadgets – children move on.

Marks

Any five clear points. One mark for each point.

Exam section 2: Critical Reading

Critical Essay

For this part of this paper you have to be prepared to write an essay on one of the texts that you have studied in class. There are five sections of questions. You have to choose one question from any section. The question you choose has to be from a section that is different from the one you picked for your Scottish Texts answers, however. In other words, you can't answer on a play in the Scottish Texts section and then answer on a play again in the Critical Essay section (even if it is a different play).

The Drama section

Let's stick with plays. Suppose you have studied a play in class, perhaps *Macbeth* by William Shakespeare. What kind of questions would you expect to come up in an exam paper about *Macbeth*? Well, first of all, there will not be a question specifically about *Macbeth* itself. In the Scottish Texts section the texts are named and specified, but this is not the case in the Critical Essay section. There will be questions about plays in general. Your first task is to find a question that fits your knowledge of the play you have studied. Don't worry too much about this. The exam is not designed to catch you out here. The questions in the exam paper should be open enough to include pretty much any text you might have studied in class. In each section there are two questions. You should be able to find a question that suits you from these two questions.

William Shakespeare

What kind of questions would you expect to see in the Drama section? Here are the main ones.

Key points !

* Questions about characters – main characters, characters who change, characters who learn something, characters who make mistakes, characters who are good/evil, and so on.
* Questions about conflict – drama is all about conflict; expect questions about conflict between main characters, between groups of people, between a main character and the other characters/the society he lives in, and so on. ⇨

* Questions about a theme or an issue – for example, love, death, ambition, greed.
* Questions about a part of the play – the beginning, the ending, a turning point.

Your knowledge of *Macbeth*

Let's look in more detail at *Macbeth* as an example of a play for the Drama section of the exam. What do you need to know about the play as you go into the exam?

You need to have a good idea of what happens in the play. You should be able to express this in a clear, concise way. Something like this:

Example

Macbeth is about a Scottish general, a well-respected soldier, who, tempted by a group of witches, and encouraged by his wife, kills the King of Scotland (Duncan) in order to become king himself. He quickly becomes obsessed with keeping the power he has gained, killing his best friend, Banquo, and killing the family of his main rival, Macduff. As his obsession with power takes hold he becomes more and more isolated from his wife, and relies on the words of the three witches (who started him on his journey to power). He takes the words of the witches on face value and feels almost protected, invulnerable because of them. Here he makes a fatal mistake. He becomes increasingly out of touch with the people around him and his country suffers. After being wronged by Macbeth, Macduff goes to England and persuades Malcolm, the son of the former king, to join forces and attack Macbeth. This he does and Macbeth is defeated and deserted by his followers, the witches' prophecies of protection crashing down, one by one.

Now that you have this knowledge in your head you need to be able to use it in a way that is relevant to the question. You need to be able to manipulate your material – to think.

Exam-style questions

Here are the two questions that are included in the specimen paper (that is, the published example) for English National 5 on the SQA website.

1 Choose a play that you feel has a turning point.
   Describe briefly what happens at this turning point and then, by referring to appropriate techniques, go on to explain how it makes an impact on the play as a whole.
2 Choose a play in which the playwright presents a flawed character who you feel is more worthy of our sympathy than criticism.
   By referring to appropriate techniques, show how the character's flawed nature is revealed, then explain how, despite this, we are led to feel sympathy for her/him.

Remember

Thinking skills are vital in English! In the exam you have to be able, first of all, to recognise a question as being suitable for the play (or poem or story) that you have studied, and then you have to be able to sort your knowledge, and think about which things you must mention, and which things are perhaps not so important.

Would these questions work for *Macbeth*? Yes, they would – both of them. For the first one, the turning point, you would have more than one possibility: the moment when Macbeth murders Duncan – it all changes after that; the moment when Macbeth arranges for his best friend, Banquo, to be killed – his obsession with power rises uncontrollably from that moment on.

And the second question? Macbeth is definitely a flawed, imperfect character. Is he worthy of our sympathy? People certainly said good things about him at the start of the play. He is referred to as 'brave Macbeth' and 'worthy gentleman'. He certainly makes mistakes, but can we understand that a lot of this is due to his wife's powers of persuasion, and the tempting promises of the witches? Can we sympathise with him when he is left with nothing at the end?

 Key points

* Notice how the questions on page 61 are constructed. You are asked to identify something in the play (a turning point, a flawed character). Then you are asked to do something with that identification: explain how the turning point has an impact on the play as a whole; show how the flawed character's nature is revealed, and how we, for one reason or another, sympathise with him/her.
* Notice also the expression 'by referring to appropriate techniques'. As soon as you see this, you perhaps think that 'appropriate techniques' has to mean things like word choice, similes, metaphors, alliteration or personification. In a large text like *Macbeth* (or a novel), however, it would be more appropriate to talk about 'bigger' techniques, such as characterisation, plot, dramatic irony, turning point or setting.

How to go about writing a critical essay

Let's take one of the two examples of questions given on page 61. Let's try the first one – the turning point. The main thing when writing a critical essay on literature you have studied is to answer the question. That is what a marker is looking for – does the essay answer the question? Is it relevant? Perhaps the most common 'fault' or 'weakness' in a critical essay is lack of relevance, of straying from the point. The best way to ensure that your essay is relevant to the question is to have a clear idea where you are going with your essay, and what you are going to say: in other words, your own plan.

How to plan an essay quickly in the exam

You might be thinking – yes, I know a plan is meant to be a good idea, but in the exam I just don't have time for that. I would say again, however, that if you don't have a plan there is a big danger that your essay will wander off the point, and you will come to the end and realise there were things you should have mentioned earlier on.

Why not try this approach? Looking at the essay question, try to think of six (or round about six) things from the play that you think you would definitely say in answer to it. These six, or so, things become the paragraphs of your essay. You could write this short list of things on your exam paper beside the question you have chosen. The list can then act as a reminder to you – it is a plan, a structure for your essay.

Trying it out – *Macbeth*

If we take Question 1 as our example, we have to, first of all, identify a turning point in the play. A few possibilities are mentioned above. Let's go for the murder of Macbeth's friend Banquo as being the turning point. That's the first task done. A relevant selection has been made. Now for the essay. Which six or so relevant points from the play would make up our essay?

Example ⚑

- Macbeth starts out the play as a hero – he tackles the traitors and fights loyally for the king to defeat the invading army from Norway. But, Macbeth meets three witches who predict great things for Macbeth, and in the future for Banquo's descendants.
- Macbeth is initially unsure, but is persuaded to murder the existing king (Duncan) by his wife.
- Macbeth feels great guilt, and there is a moment when we think he might stop his murderous behaviour here, but this soon changes as he turns his attention to Banquo (who knows too much and has also been promised much by the witches).
- Macbeth hires murderers to kill Banquo. He does this without his wife's knowledge/help. (We can see the reasons, 'justifications' for killing Duncan, but this is surely too far. It all changes for Macbeth from this point on.)
- Macbeth returns to the witches who make further statements related to Macbeth's safety (or otherwise). ⇨

- Macbeth acts on the witches' statements in a bloody way, killing Macduff's family and, in doing this, creating a deadly enemy. He is now acting alone, moving further and further away from his wife and trusted friends.
- Macbeth loses everything – his wife dies, he is isolated, and is ultimately defeated by Macduff and Malcolm. He has been on a downward slope ever since he was confirmed as a cold-bloodied killer when he has Banquo killed.

Now you have six or seven points from the play. They are all relevant to the turning point – what has led up to it, and what happens for the main characters afterwards. If you referred to all of them in your essay you would have a decent, relevant essay.

How to begin your essay

The opening paragraph is very important because it has a crucial part to play in helping you to set out your stall in terms of what you are going to say in response to the question. It helps to establish relevance right from the start.

There are usually three essential items in an introduction:
- Selection – state the text and author that you are going to answer on and establish relevance to the question.
- Setting the context – a little on what the play is mainly about/ concerned with (in terms of themes).
- Answer to the question – a short, simple response to the question.

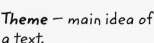

Remember

Theme – *main idea of a text.*

Let's try this approach with our text and question. An introduction for an essay on *Macbeth* in answer to Question 1 on page 61 might go something like this:

Example

A play that has a clear turning point is 'Macbeth' by William Shakespeare. Macbeth is a well-respected Scottish general who becomes too ambitious and kills the king in order to become the king. The turning point of the play happens when Macbeth arranges the death of his close friend Banquo, showing that he is becoming obsessed with power and greed. Macbeth has clearly changed. In this play Shakespeare explores ideas of ambition, greed and loyalty.

Having written your introduction, the remainder of your essay should be the six or seven points identified above. Through these points you will be able to demonstrate what has led up to the turning point, the turning point itself, and the consequences of the turning point.

Writing in paragraphs

You must remember to write in paragraphs. Paragraphs help you to structure your essay. Having identified six or seven key points to mention, you have already established a paragraph structure.

The structure of each paragraph

This will obviously depend on what you want to say in each paragraph, but remember to make sure that all is relevant to the question. Try using this approach:

- Point – a statement or point relevant to the question, in the form of a topic sentence.
- Evidence – a quotation, or reference to something from the play that supports your point.
- Evaluation/Explanation – comments from you on the evidence that you have provided, again relevant to the question, and making reference to techniques (such as characterisation, language or plot, for example).
- (You can add an 'L' to the pattern. 'L' is for 'Link,' and you can try to link the final sentence of your paragraph with the first one of the next paragraph.)

Let's try this out:

Example

Just before the turning point, it seems as if Macbeth has regretted what he has done, and will be able to control his ambition (one of the main themes of the play). He seems appalled by his actions, and we don't expect him to kill again. We think this when he looks at his blood-stained hands (after killing Duncan), and says:

> 'Will all Neptune's Ocean wash this blood
>
> clean from my hand?'

He reckons that it would take all the water from the sea to wash the blood of murder off his hands. He then goes further and says that it wouldn't – the sea would actually change colour, from green to red. This shows the huge amount of guilt he is feeling, if he thinks the blood on his hands would be so hard to remove. At this point in the play we think that, following the murder of Duncan, Macbeth has regretted his actions and that there is no way he would murder again. The turning point changes our view of Macbeth again, however …

Your essay could be made up of six or seven paragraphs like this.

Conclusion

Make sure the marker knows that you are rounding off your essay by starting your concluding paragraph with signalling words, like 'In conclusion', 'Finally', 'To sum up', for example. In your conclusion, try to sum up your main thoughts in answer to the key words of the question. In this case, why was the turning point so important for our understanding of Macbeth, and the other main characters in the play? Try also to refer to the themes or main ideas of the play. (Note that it is a good idea to keep mentioning themes throughout your essay, as in the example paragraph above.)

Quotes

Everyone worries about this aspect of writing a critical essay in an exam. How many quotes do you need? Which quotes should I learn? What if I make a mistake with a quote?

It is really hard to put a figure on a number of quotes to learn. You will need to learn some, as you would be expected to include some in an essay on a play. If you stick to the six-or-seven-main-paragraphs idea above, you might think that implies one quote per paragraph. Yes, but some paragraphs could need several quotes, and some none. Either way, you will need to have a range of quotes to select from, depending on the question. In a great play like *Macbeth*, in which every line seems to be full of meaning and importance, it is quite a task to try to narrow down a list of 'essential' quotes. Here's my attempt:

Macbeth quotes

- 'Fair is foul, and foul is fair' – Witches
- 'Brave Macbeth … he unseam'd him from the nave to the chops
  And fixed his head upon our battlements' – Captain
- 'O valiant cousin, worthy gentleman' – Duncan (talking about Macbeth)
- 'What he hath lost, noble Macbeth hath won' – Duncan
- 'so foul and fair a day I have not seen' – Macbeth (these are his first words and they link Macbeth with the words of the witches)
- 'Lesser than Macbeth, and greater' – Witches (comparing Banquo with Macbeth)
- 'Glamis, and Thane of Cawdor!
  The greatest is behind' – Macbeth
- 'Whose horrid image doth unfix my hair,
  And make my seated heart knock at my ribs' – Macbeth (first thinks about killing the king)
- 'If chance will have me King,
  Why chance may crown me without my stir' – Macbeth
- 'stars hide your fires
  Let not light see my black and deep desires' – Macbeth
- 'Yet I do fear thy nature
  It is too full of the milk of human kindness
  To catch the nearest way' – Lady Macbeth (reading Macbeth's letter telling her of his meeting with the witches)
- 'Look like the innocent flower, but be the serpent under it' – Lady Macbeth (to Macbeth)
- 'If it were done, when 'tis done, then 'twere well,
  If it were done quickly' – Macbeth (thinking about the murder)

> **Remember**
>
> I have given you an idea of how to structure an essay above. But please remember there is no single structure for writing a critical essay. You can follow your own pattern, as long as it is relevant to the question. As I have said before, thinking skills are central to English, and if your thinking doesn't fit the essay plans that people suggest to you, then don't use them. The main thing is to keep your essay relevant to the question.

⇒

- 'We will proceed no further in this business' – Macbeth (makes clear he doesn't want to commit murder)
- 'Live a coward in thine own esteem' – Lady Macbeth (tries to persuade Macbeth that he should kill Duncan)
- 'Bring forth men-children only' – Macbeth (shocked at how brutal Lady Macbeth seems capable of being)
- 'False face must hide what the false heart doth know' – Macbeth
- 'Is this a dagger which I see before me?' – Macbeth (is he now 'seeing things'?)
- 'Had he not resembled my father as he slept, I had done it' – Lady Macbeth (admits she couldn't kill the king herself)
- 'Macbeth shall sleep no more' – Macbeth (just after killing the king Macbeth is worried that he has heard a voice saying this)
- 'Will all great Neptune's Ocean wash this blood
  Clean from my hand?' – Macbeth (worried he will not be able to get over the guilt of killing the king)
- 'My hands are of your colour: but I shame to wear a heart so white' – Lady Macbeth (she says she has blood on her hands too but is not a coward ['white'])
- 'Wake Duncan with thy knocking: I would thou could' – Macbeth (regrets killing Duncan)
- 'Where we are, there's daggers in men's smiles' – Donalbain (explaining what has happened to Scotland – it has become unsafe for him and his brother, who are the sons of Duncan)
- 'Thou has it now, King, Cawdor, Glamis, all
  And I fear thou played most foully for it' – Banquo (suspects Macbeth has killed Duncan)
- 'O full of scorpions is my mind, dear wife' – Macbeth (makes it clear that he is paranoid/anxious)
- 'Thou canst not say I did it: never shake thy gory locks at me' – Macbeth (at party sees Banquo's ghost)
- 'From this moment
  The very firstlings of my heart shall be
  The firstlings of my hand' – Macbeth (after seeing the witches says he will act first and think later)
- 'Out damned spot' – Lady Macbeth (sleepwalking and overcome by guilt; she now thinks she can't remove blood from her hands)
- 'Here's the smell of blood still: all the perfumes of Arabia will not sweeten this little hand' – Lady Macbeth (as above)
- 'I have almost forgot the taste of fears' – Macbeth
- 'Tomorrow and tomorrow and tomorrow …' – Macbeth's speech after the death of his wife – look at it again, it shows Macbeth's growing despair
- 'Turn hell-hound, turn' – Macduff (prepares to fight Macbeth)
- 'I will not yield to kiss the ground before young Malcolm's feet' – Macbeth (he fights to the last)
- 'This dead butcher and his fiend-like Queen' – Malcolm (passes judgement on Macbeth)

How will my essay be marked, and what is the marker looking for?

Your essay will be marked out of 20. There are three 'pass' categories: Category 3 (10–13 marks), Category 2 (14–17 marks), Category 1 (18–20 marks). In short, the categories are described in these terms:

● Category 1 – Very good (thorough and precise).
● Category 2 – Good (very detailed and shows some insight).
● Category 3 – Satisfactory (fairly detailed and relevant).

An essay that falls below the 'pass' mark of 10 out of 20 would do so because it lacked detail and relevance; it may also be superficial in analysis and technically weak in the way it is written.

The marker is looking for an essay that shows understanding of the text, that contains analysis of the techniques used by the writer, that contains a reaction to the effect of the text, and that is well-organised and clearly written.

More detailed information about the marking of essays can be easily found on the SQA website (following the links for English National 5, Specimen Paper).

The Prose section

Let's now look at another text, this time from the Prose section – *To Kill A Mockingbird* by Harper Lee.

Exam-style questions

Here are the Prose questions from the Specimen English National 5 Critical Reading paper.

1 Choose a novel or a short story or a work of non-fiction that explores an important theme.
By referring to appropriate techniques, show how the author has explored this theme.

2 Choose a novel or a short story in which the author creates a fascinating character.
By referring to appropriate techniques, show how the author has created this character and why you found him/her so fascinating.

Key points

Note that the Critical Essay questions contain the expression 'By referring to appropriate techniques'. This is an important point because 'appropriate techniques' will not be the same for Prose or Drama or Poetry. For example, it will be much more important to provide quotes in a Drama or Poetry essay, but less so for Prose. If you are writing about a novel (such as *To Kill A Mockingbird*), you will be dealing more with key episodes, characterisation and setting, and less with word choice, imagery, and so on.

Going back to the questions above, you will see that both questions would work very well for *To Kill A Mockingbird*. There are clear themes in the book: prejudice, racism, growing up and isolation to name a few. There are definitely fascinating characters: Scout (the narrator of the book), Atticus (Scout's father and the lawyer who defends Tom Robinson in a controversial case), Boo Radley (the mysterious recluse).

Still from the film of *To Kill a Mockingbird* (1962)

If you chose the first question you would have to decide on a theme and then think about which key incidents from the book really help to put across that theme.

Say you pick the theme of growing up. You would probably focus mostly on the character of Scout as she tells us the story. It is her version of events that we hear; it is her voice that we listen to. This could be the first point of your essay! Which moments from the book would you focus on as key incidents?

 Activity

If you know the novel, which key incidents would you select to demonstrate the theme of growing up (especially with reference to Scout)?

Answers

Did you go for any of these?
- Scout's early fascination with Boo Radley. She is initially scared of him. She lacks knowledge of him. She rolls up to his house in a tyre.

⇨

- Boo Radley leaves presents for Scout and her brother in a tree. Her (slowly) growing awareness that Boo Radley is not what she first thought of him.
- The fire in the street. Boo Radley puts a blanket round Scout's shoulders.
- Scout's initial thoughts about her father – that he is boring, for example – start to change when he shoots the mad dog.
- Scout's growing awareness of the people in the town – the people at school, the Cunninghams.
- What she learns of her father through the court case – initial abuse, then she intervenes to help her father outside the courthouse.
- Her growing awareness of the lives of black people through a visit to their church.
- Her changing views on Aunt Alexandra – how her views change from objecting to her aunt's determination to 'make her a girl' through wearing dresses, to Scout's later appreciation of her as being a 'lady' after her aunt comes round to Atticus' views on Tom Robinson.
- Boo Radley saves Scout's life from the evil Bob Ewell. She knows more about him, but realises she will never see him again.

These are just a few, but you can see that these incidents are all closely related to the themes of the book. They also allow you to discuss points on characterisation and setting. This is all analysis, and exactly what you have to do for a critical essay.

Quotes for prose texts

As I said above, quotes are far less important in an essay on a large prose text. You would want to have a few significant quotes ready to use where appropriate, however. For example, for *To Kill A Mockingbird*, you would want to remember Scout's father Atticus' key statement:

You never really understand a person until you consider things from his point of view … until you climb into his skin and walk around in it.

Critical Reading in other genres

The two examples discussed in detail above relate to the first two sections of the Critical Essay section of the Critical Reading paper. There are three further sections: Poetry, Film and TV Drama, and Language Study. The approach to writing critical essays on texts from these sections is essentially the same as described above. The main thing is to try to make sure your essay answers the question. While answering the question you must try to show your understanding of the text(s) you have studied. You must also try to analyse the ways in which the text is put together

– how it works. To analyse effectively, you must make reference to parts of the text, explain how they work, and comment on how they contribute to meaning.

Many people like to write about poetry in exams because they feel that they can handle the material more easily – perhaps they can remember (or memorise) a whole poem. But don't be frightened of the larger texts – as long as you have a good idea of what happens, can pick out the important episodes, and know how the characters relate to each other, you will be able to write a decent critical essay. Hopefully, you will find the material in Chapter 6 (on Scottish Texts) helpful in your study of poetry. Questions on poetry are found in Section C of the paper.

As examples of longer texts we looked at *Macbeth* and *To Kill A Mockingbird*. It is just as valid to study a media text, and attempt a question from the Film and TV Drama section (Section D). You should expect two types of question in this section. One will ask you to select a key scene from your choice of film or TV drama. The question will ask you to analyse this scene, and go on to show how the scene relates to the rest of the film or TV drama. The other question will ask you about the whole text, perhaps concentrating on genre or conflict, or an issue, and so on. Some people think that you have to fill an essay from this section with very technical media analysis. Yes, media analysis does have a vocabulary of its own (and some of them are listed in the box at the top of the section in the exam paper), but remember that this is an English exam and that techniques like characterisation and plot are relevant here too.

Section E (Language Study) is much more specialised, but again requires you to show your understanding and skills of analysis in a discussion of texts selected by you. To answer a question from this section, you would need to come prepared with evidence from projects you had done on language. There are essentially two types of question: one concentrating on advertisements; the other on language spoken or used by groups of people (for example, people with the same job, the same hobby, or from the same part of the country).

Remember

☞ For the Critical Reading paper you have to be prepared to write one Critical Essay.
☞ When selecting an essay question, make sure it is not the same genre/text as your option for the Scottish Texts section.
☞ Plan your essay before you start to write – jot down six or seven points that you definitely will make.
☞ Keep your essay relevant to the question. Refer to the words of the question throughout your essay. This will help you keep it relevant.
☞ Quotes are necessary for Drama and Poetry, less so for Prose.
☞ Show your thinking skills in the Critical Essay.

Chapter 6
Scottish Texts

In the second paper of your exam you have to be prepared to answer questions on a Scottish text. There is a list of authors and set texts from these authors on the SQA website. One list is for National 5 English and the other for Higher English. There is cross-over between the two lists: some authors and texts are on both. To prepare for this you will have studied at least one writer from the list in detail with your teacher. In this chapter I shall look at one of the most popular authors, Norman MacCaig, and try to show you the kind of questions to expect. Then I will move on to looking at another Scottish writer, this time of drama: Ann Marie Di Mambro, and again try to show you the kind of questions to expect.

Norman MacCaig

Norman MacCaig is great. In Scotland, we should be proud of him. He was born in 1910 and lived most of his life in Edinburgh; however, he had family connections with the Highlands, and spent a good deal of time there. In some ways, therefore, his idea of Scotland spanned the length of the country.

Norman MacCaig

In this chapter, we shall look at two poems by MacCaig with a view towards answering set text questions on them. On first impressions these two poems seem to be quite different, but after a closer look, we will see that they have many similarities. This is what you need to keep in mind for the Scottish Texts section of the exam.

Key points

* In the exam you will be given a whole text or part of a text from the set writers. You will be expected to answer questions on the text provided, and to be able to relate the ideas and language of that text to at least one of the other specified texts from that writer.
* You are guaranteed a complete printed text (or extract) from the writer you have prepared. You don't know which text the exam will produce, however. If you have prepared Norman MacCaig, there are six of his poems on the list, any one of which could come up in the exam. The last question in the exam will ask you to compare the printed poem with (at least) one other poem from the list. So it is a good idea, when you are studying a writer for this part of the exam, to look for, or be thinking of, connections between the texts. This last question is worth 8 marks (out of the 20 available). It is best to be prepared for it.

I've picked the two most popular poems from the list on the SQA website ('Basking Shark' and 'Assisi'). Let's now have a look at them with a view towards the kind of questions to expect, and also with an eye on connections between them.

On the face of it, these two poems are very different: one is about a shark and the other about a visit to a church in Italy. As you become familiar with them, however, you will see similarities in the way they are written (both are written from the point of view of a poet or persona addressing the reader with his thoughts), and in subject matter/themes.

Both poems seem to involve the poet thinking about/reflecting on an experience. 'Basking Shark' is about a close encounter with the huge, harmless shark that can sometimes be seen off the coasts of Scotland. 'Assisi' describes a visit to the Basilica of St Francis of Assisi, the church built in honour of St Francis, in Assisi, Italy. People often ask – why do people write poems? One answer is that poets write about what they see, what they have experienced. This seems to be true of MacCaig – he notices things. He describes experiences and then reflects on their meaning. In many ways he celebrates things, preserves the memory of them. So, what did he see? What did he notice when he wrote 'Basking Shark' and 'Assisi'?

Basking Shark

To stub an oar on a rock where none should be,

To have it rise with a slounge out of the sea

Is a thing that happened once (too often) to me.

But not too often – though enough. I count as gain

5   That once I met, on a sea tin-tacked with rain,

That roomsized monster with a matchbox brain.

He displaced more than water. He shoggled me

Centuries back – this decadent townee

Shook on a wrong branch of his family tree.

10 Swish up the dirt and, when it settles, a spring

Is all the clearer. I saw me, in one fling,

Emerging from the slime of everything.

So who's the monster? The thought made me grow pale

For twenty seconds while, sail after sail,

15 The tall fin slid away and then the tail.

Norman MacCaig

To stub an oar on a rock where none should be

This is the first line of the poem and leads us straight into MacCaig's experience, and it's a pretty memorable experience. He is on a boat at sea (presumably not far from the shore as he is using oars), and his oar hits not a rock but a living thing – he identifies it as a basking shark. (It is interesting that MacCaig uses the word 'stub', as in to 'stub out a cigarette'. He was a very stubborn smoker.) Now, to see a shark at all would be an amazing thing, but to see one in Scotland, and to be so close to it is clearly something to remember.

What do we know about basking sharks? First of all, they are huge (up to ten metres long!). They are one of the largest sharks in the world, but they are completely harmless – they feed on tiny plankton. They are filter feeders, and have a huge mouth that opens to take in great gulps of sea water, hopefully full of plankton. They move very slowly – only three miles per hour (slightly slower than walking pace!). In the summer they come quite close to shore and 'bask' at the surface with their mouths open to feed. What exactly does 'bask' mean? According to the Concise Oxford Dictionary, 'bask' means to 'lie exposed to warmth and sunlight for pleasure'. This fits with MacCaig's next description of the shark:

To have it rise with a slounge out of the sea

Here he notices the shark's leisurely movements. The word 'slounge' makes that very clear. It means 'to hang about in a lazy, slouching manner'. Think of 'lounge' and 'lounging'. This perhaps surprising, relaxed manner and behaviour of the shark makes an impression on MacCaig. He tells us that this, 'Is a thing that happened once (too often) to me.' Maybe the expression '(too often)' added as an aside in brackets suggests that he was a little bit unnerved by the experience, that it shook him a up a bit. This impression seems to be confirmed by the next line: 'But not too often – though enough.' But he is pleased that this has happened to him, that he has seen it: 'I count as gain / that once I met'. In this way MacCaig celebrates the experience, celebrates nature.

Next there is brilliant description of what happened and how MacCaig reacted to it. He introduces a great image to describe the surface of the water: 'on a sea tin-tacked with rain'. Here he compares the little holes drilled by rain into the still surface of the water to tacks being hammered into a tin plate. You can imagine it. He goes on to provide a second great image in a description of the shark itself: 'That roomsized monster with a matchbox brain.' The massive scale of the shark clearly comes across (as big as a room); it is like a monster (monstrous) in size. But, MacCaig reminds us, it is big in size, but small in brain size/development. It is impressively huge, but not in all aspects. The word 'matchbox' makes an effective contrast with 'roomsized'. Some aspects of the shark are huge and impressive; some are not. In comparison with basking sharks, humans might not be as large in size, but they have bigger brains.

Next comes a real turning point in the poem, in the poet's reflection on the experience. MacCaig writes 'He displaced more than water.' The shark's weight has moved and upset the water, but it has also moved and upset the writer. The shark has prompted MacCaig to think about our own origins as human beings, 'Emerging from the slime of everything.' He sees a connection between the shark and humans: we have all come from the same place, the 'slime' of our evolutionary origins. Notice again MacCaig's reaction to this thought: it has unsettled him. The word 'shoggled' means 'shook' or 'cause to move', and suggests that MacCaig has been unnerved by his encounter with the shark. He uses another image to put across the power of this unsettling experience:

Swish up the dirt and, when it settles, a spring

Is all the clearer.

Here MacCaig compares his experience to stirring up a pool of water in the mountains. Initially it will be cloudy with dirt/sediment, but after a few moments it will become clear (he suggests clearer than before). He is suggesting it is the same with our thoughts/ideas. Stir them up from time to time and they will become clearer. In other words, use your brain to think about things!

In the final stanza of the poem, MacCaig tries to draw a conclusion from the experience. Having recognised similarities between the shark and himself, he thinks again about a word he has used earlier in the poem – 'monster'. He asks simply:

So who's the monster?

At first, MacCaig had been overwhelmed by the size of the shark and had called it immediately a 'monster'. Now he has considered the experience more deeply, however, and has acknowledged similarities, he has had to reconsider his use of the word 'monster'. In asking the question above, there is a clear sense that MacCaig is allowing for the possibility that humans could be called 'monsters' too, not monsters in size, but possibly in actions. Is human behaviour not monstrous at times? MacCaig is again unsettled by this thought. He writes, 'The thought made me grow pale'. It is only a passing thought, however ('For twenty seconds'). But a much larger frame of time is suggested as the shark slowly goes by:

For twenty seconds while, sail after sail,

The tall fin slid away and then the tail.

The repetition of the word 'sail' plus the rhyme with 'tail' creates the impression that the shark took an age to pass the watching poet. There are other layers of meaning in this ending: the glimpse back into prehistoric time that the shark has given him, and a reminder of our common origins.

Activity

Having looked closely at the poem, what could MacCaig's concerns/ themes be?

Answer

There is obviously something about the value of experience, of noticing our surroundings and thinking about them. In this way the poem is a celebration of our surroundings, in this case about an aspect of nature. There also seems to be something here about what it means to be human or, in a sense, imperfectly human (remember the question 'so who's the monster?').

Let's move on to 'Assisi' and see if there are similarities.

Assisi

The dwarf with his hands on backwards

sat, slumped like a half-filled sack

on tiny twisted legs from which

sawdust might run,

5   outside the three tiers of churches built

in honour of St Francis, brother

of the poor, talker with birds, over whom

he had the advantage

of not being dead yet.

10 A priest explained

how clever it was of Giotto

to make his frescoes tell stories

that would reveal to the illiterate the goodness

of God and the suffering

15 of His Son. I understood

the explanation and

the cleverness.

A rush of tourists, clucking contentedly,

fluttered after him as he scattered

20 the grain of the Word. It was they who had passed

the ruined temple outside, whose eyes

wept pus, whose back was higher

than his head, whose lopsided mouth

said Grazie in a voice as sweet

25 as a child's when she speaks to her mother

or a bird's when it spoke

to St Francis.

Norman MacCaig

As with 'Basking Shark' this poem begins with an experience. The poet tells us of a visit to the Italian city of Assisi and, in particular, the Basilica of St Francis (the huge church built in memory of St Francis).

Before we look at the poem we should find out a little about St Francis. He lived in Italy between 1181 (or 1182) and 1226. His father was a clothes merchant, and Francis grew up fairly comfortably off. As a teenager he hung around with a gang of boys and partied as much as the rest of his friends. At the end of his teenage years he became a soldier and saw some conflict. He spent some time in prison, and there he changed. He lost his taste for partying and began, instead, to pray. His new-found religious feelings did not go down well with his father and, at the age of 25, Francis gave away all his money and belongings, leaving a pile of clothes at his father's feet. God would be his father from now on, he said.

He began to preach and adopted a strange style: he would dance and make animal noises; he wore a filthy tunic with a rope as a belt. He hung around with lepers (the real social outcasts of the time). People thought he was mad and dangerous. They threw mud at him. But he was a very sweet, kind man and he clearly had charisma. It was not long before people began to be drawn to him. Church bells rang when he came to town, and crowds gathered. People began to talk of him as a saint. In 1224 he received the stigmata (the wounds of Christ). Flesh seemed to emerge from either sides of his hands and feet, resembling nails as in Christ's crucifixion. For the people of Assisi this confirmed Francis' sainthood. As soon as he died (after horrible illness and suffering, still living in absolute poverty), the church of St Francis was built in his honour. It is a huge structure – two levels above ground and a crypt underground, where St Francis is buried. The lavish, hugely expensive, memorial to him stood, of course, in complete contradiction to all that Francis stood for – a simple life, without money or possessions.

MacCaig does not start his poem 'Assisi' with St Francis or the church, he starts with a beggar sitting outside. MacCaig does not want us to think first of all of the beauty and grandeur of the church, he wants us to think of a man who is described in shocking, unsentimental terms:

The dwarf with his hands on backwards

sat, slumped like a half-filled sack

on tiny twisted legs from which

sawdust might run,

The word choice here conveys suffering – 'slumped' gives the idea of not having the strength to stand up, or of being in a decline; 'twisted' suggests not functioning. The image of the 'half-filled sack' emphasises what is not there for the man, what is missing for him.

Knowing what we do about St Francis, however, would he not be interested in this man? Immediately following this, MacCaig sets up a contrast with the lavishly built church: 'outside the three tiers of churches built / in honour of St Francis'. The contrast is clear – the church is extended and full in size, the beggar outside is 'half-filled'. MacCaig makes the connection between St Francis and the beggar: 'in honour of St Francis, brother / of the poor'. Irony is apparent here – the lavish church and the poor beggar. MacCaig adds to the irony by saying that the beggar has one 'advantage' over St Francis, 'not being dead yet.' It doesn't sound much of an advantage.

In the second stanza MacCaig turns his attention to the famous paintings by Giotto on the wall of the Church of St Francis. He tells us that, on his visit, a priest explained that the purpose of these paintings was to:

tell stories

that would reveal to the illiterate the goodness

of God and the suffering

of His Son.

In MacCaig's hugely understated reaction, 'I understood / the explanation and / the cleverness', we have an ambiguity (an uncertainty, a doubt). What exactly has he understood? The genuine skill of the painter? Or the cleverness of the church, the priests, in putting across, through the paintings, the message that they want people to hear?

Next comes the famous image of the 'tourists' who follow the priest on his tour 'clucking contentedly' (like birds? chickens? notice the alliteration used to draw attention to this description). They 'fluttered after him as he scattered / the grain of the Word.' Now, there is a sense here in the word 'grain' that the priest is feeding the tourists what he wants to give them, what it suits him to hand out. The tourists are happy ('contentedly') to hear it. The whole image of 'feeding' the tourists is ironic, too, of course, if you consider the hungry beggar outside. And MacCaig takes us back to him in a description that is even more horrible:

whose eyes

wept pus, whose back was higher

than his head, whose lopsided mouth …

The poet moves to the end of the poem with further contrasts. The beggar is again contrasted with the grand church – he is a 'ruined temple'. This contrasts with the substantial 'three tiers of churches built / in honour of St Francis'. MacCaig then sets up a further contrast involving the beggar, however – a contrast of expectations. Having just been told that his mouth is 'lopsided', MacCaig lets us know that he:

said Grazie in a voice as sweet

as a child's when she speaks to her mother

or a bird's when it spoke

to St Francis.

This cuts across the horrible descriptions of the beggar and gives him a sweetness that links him with St Francis – St Francis himself was said to be sweet-natured and generous, and St Francis was (as MacCaig has already told us) a 'talker with birds'. The tourists have been associated with birds ('clucking contentedly'), but MacCaig is ending his poem by hinting that the true associations are between St Francis and the beggar on one hand, and the priest and the tourists (both ignoring the beggar) on the other.

At the end of the poem we are left with questions. Who does the beggar thank? Have the tourists all ignored him? Is MacCaig angry at what he has seen? Or is he unsure what to make of it? Is he recording the contrasts and contradictions as he sees them? Or is this an attack on human hypocrisy and cruelty? Think about the poem 'Basking Shark' and its ending, 'So who's the monster? The thought made me grow pale'. Who is the monster in 'Assisi'? The beggar is described in monstrous terms, but he is clearly not to be thought of as such ('in a voice as sweet / as a child's'). Is the priest a monster for doing nothing about the beggar's poverty? Are the tourists monsters for ignoring the beggar? But do they all ignore him? Is it in any way 'wrong' to admire the achievement of Giotto in painting his masterpieces?

Perhaps all of these questions lead us to consider similarities in theme between this poem and 'Basking Shark'.

Activity

What are the similarities in theme between 'Basking Shark' and 'Assisi'?

Answer

Both poems are a result of experiences, or observations about aspects of life. Both involve some reflection (thinking) about what has happened/what the poet has seen. Both seem to be about the human condition – what it means to be human; how humans are, in some ways, imperfect.

Exam practice

Now for the exam questions.

What kind of questions should you expect to see in the Scottish Texts section? What follows are two sets of questions and answers. One for 'Basking Shark', and one for 'Assisi'.

Exam-style questions

Read the poem 'Basking Shark' (given again below for your reference) and then attempt the following questions.

1 This poem seems to have come from personal experience.
   Summarise the key points of this experience and how the poet is affected by it. You should make four key points in your answer. (4 marks) ⇨

2 What value does the poet place on this experience?
Answer with reference to the poem. (2 marks)

3 Identify two examples of imagery from the poem and explain their effectiveness. (4 marks)

4 How effective do you find the final stanza as a conclusion to the poem?
Your answer might deal with ideas and/or language. (2 marks)

5 With close textual reference, show how the ideas and/or language of this poem are similar or different to the ideas and/or language from at least one other poem by MacCaig which you have read. (8 marks)

Basking Shark

To stub an oar on a rock where none should be,

To have it rise with a slounge out of the sea

Is a thing that happened once (too often) to me.

But not too often – though enough. I count as gain

5   That once I met, on a sea tin-tacked with rain,

That roomsized monster with a matchbox brain.

He displaced more than water. He shoggled me

Centuries back – this decadent townee

Shook on a wrong branch of his family tree.

10   Swish up the dirt and, when it settles, a spring

Is all the clearer. I saw me, in one fling,

Emerging from the slime of everything.

So who's the monster? The thought made me grow pale

For twenty seconds while, sail after sail,

15   The tall fin slid away and then the tail.

Norman MacCaig

Answer

1 This poem seems to have come from personal experience.
Summarise the key points of this experience and how the poet is affected by it. You should make four key points in your answer.
(4 marks)

This is a skill with which you will now be familiar. It is an essential part of your National 5 English toolkit. Try to isolate at least three main points from the poem. Remember that main points only are required. Leave out examples and supporting detail.

Answers

Examples of acceptable points:

- The poet encounters a shark (at sea).
- This is an unusual/noteworthy experience for him.
- It causes him to think of his origins (as a human being).
- It causes him to think about what it is to be human/animal.
- It causes him to consider a value judgement in a comparison between humans and creatures.

Marks

Four clear points would achieve four marks. One mark for each clear point offered.

Answer

2 What value does the poet place on this experience?
   Answer with reference to the poem. (2 marks)

Answers

- The poet values the experience highly. This is seen in the words, 'I count as gain'.
- The poet values the effects of the experience. This is seen when he reflects that his thinking has become 'all the clearer.'
- Poet is unsure of/disturbed by experience. This is seen in the words '(too often)' in the line 'Is a thing that happened once (too often) to me.' Or in the line 'But not too often – though enough.'

Marks

One comment plus one reference would mean two marks.

Answer

3 Identify two examples of imagery from the poem and explain their effectiveness. (4 marks)

For an imagery question at National 5 English you will sometimes be directed towards an example of imagery, or you might be asked to find some for yourself. If the imagery really stands out then the latter approach is likely. In the discussion on pages 74–75, we looked at the imagery used by MacCaig in this poem. This question should not then be too difficult. The answers are given below. ⇨

Answers

- 'sea tin-tacked with rain' – the calm/flat surface of the sea seems like metal, with raindrops drilling/hammering little holes in it.
- 'roomsized monster with a matchbox brain' – the vast size of the shark effectively conveyed through the words 'roomsized monster'. The smallness of its brain/brain development effectively conveyed by 'matchbox brain'.
- 'this decadent townee / shook on a wrong branch of his family tree' – idea of a family tree represented as a real tree that has been shaken/disturbed by his reflections on the shark/his origins.
- 'swish up the dirt and, when it settles, a spring / Is all the clearer' – the idea of a spring being clarified by stirring it up represents MacCaig's thoughts being clarified by this experience.

Marks

Two references to imagery plus two comments on their effectiveness would mean four marks.

Answer

4   How effective do you find the final stanza as a conclusion to the poem?
Your answer might deal with ideas and/or language. (2 marks)

In a question about a conclusion, think about endings. Does the conclusion tie up earlier ideas? Or does it sum up ideas? Does it leave the reader with a firm sense of an ending, or does it leave the reader with questions?

We looked closely at the ending in the discussion of the poem on pages 75–76. Have another look at that. Remember, whatever the point you decide to make, you need to back it up through reference to the text.

Answers

- 'So who's the monster?' – (rhetorical) question corresponds to one of MacCaig's central ideas/reflections in the poem: sharks and humans have come from the same origins. Do monsters always have to come from the animal kingdom? Can humans not be monsters, too?
- Also – asking an unanswered question leaves the reader thinking.
- 'The thought made me grow pale' – the word 'pale' suggests that the experience/reflection on the experience has had an effect on MacCaig; it has shaken/upset/unnerved him.
- 'For twenty seconds' – MacCaig here is pointing to the fact that the experience that he is writing about happened quickly, but it had, perhaps, a lasting effect on him. The poem is about a quick, unexpected experience that MacCaig has recorded for us.

⇨

- 'sail after sail' – the passing shark's slow movements noted here at the end of the poem are an effective echo of earlier references to the shark's slowness, for example, 'slounge'.
- As above for 'The tall fin slid away and then the tail. – comment could also be made about the age taken for the shark to pass, corresponding to the mental journey back in time that MacCaig took as a result of seeing the shark.

Marks

One mark for a relevant reference. One mark for a comment on a concluding function or comment relating to main idea of the poem.

Answer

5 With close textual reference, show how the ideas and/or language of this poem are similar or different to the ideas and/or language from at least one other poem by MacCaig which you have read. (8 marks)

In order to achieve full marks for this question you need to be able to pick out three features or ideas from this poem and then show how these features or ideas are similar to ones from at least one other poem by MacCaig from the published list. You must also be able to quote from the other poem (or poems) that you are referring to.

Answers

As we have looked at 'Assisi' in this chapter, you could make these three points of comparison:

- Subject matter – both poems are based on personal experiences; an encounter with a shark, visiting a famous church.
- Use of imagery/metaphors – both poems make use of strong imagery, for example 'roomsized monster with a matchbox brain' from 'Basking Shark', and 'A rush of tourists, clucking contentedly,' from 'Assisi'.
- Themes – 'Assisi' and 'Basking Shark' share themes – the value of experience, the human condition, what it means to be human, human imperfection.

Marks

In order to achieve full marks for this question, you must be able to identify similarities or differences in the ideas or language, or both, from this poem and, at least one other. You will be given up to two marks for making this identification, and explaining it.

⇨

You then have to make one reference to this poem (for example, to an idea or to a technique), and make a comment on it. This again is worth two marks (one mark for reference, one mark for comment).

To achieve the other four marks, you have to go on to make two further references to at least one other poem by MacCaig. You will be given one mark for each reference (for example, an idea, a technique, a relevant quote), and one mark for each supporting comment.

This adds up to eight marks.

Exam-style questions

Read the poem 'Assisi' (given again below for your reference) and then attempt the following questions.

1 Some aspects of his visit to the Church of St Francis in Assisi cause the poet concern.
Summarise his main concerns, as outlined in the poem. (3 marks)

2 Show how the poet uses contrasting word choice in stanza one to make **one** of these concerns clear. (3 marks)

3 Explain the poet's use of tone in stanza two. (2 marks)

4 Show how **two** examples of the poet's use of language in the final stanza effectively contribute to the main ideas or concerns of the poem. (4 marks)

5 With close textual reference, show how a theme (or themes) from this poem has similarity with a theme (or themes) from at least one other poem by MacCaig that you have read. (8 marks)

Assisi

The dwarf with his hands on backwards

sat, slumped like a half-filled sack

on tiny twisted legs from which

sawdust might run,

5 outside the three tiers of churches built

in honour of St Francis, brother

of the poor, talker with birds, over whom

he had the advantage

of not being dead yet.

10 A priest explained

how clever it was of Giotto

to make his frescoes tell stories

that would reveal to the illiterate the goodness

of God and the suffering

15 of His Son. I understood

the explanation and

the cleverness.

A rush of tourists, clucking contentedly,

fluttered after him as he scattered

20 the grain of the Word. It was they who had passed

the ruined temple outside, whose eyes

wept pus, whose back was higher

than his head, whose lopsided mouth

said Grazie in a voice as sweet

25 as a child's when she speaks to her mother

or a bird's when it spoke

to St Francis.

Norman MacCaig

Answer

1 Some aspects of his visit to the Church of St Francis in Assisi cause the poet concern.
Summarise his main concerns, as outlined in the poem. (3 marks)

Again, this is a summary question that assesses your understanding of the whole poem. You have to isolate the main ideas – the main issues raised by MacCaig in this poem.

Answers

- There is a poor man/beggar sitting outside a very grand church.
- The church is lavishly built, the man outside is 'ruined'.
- The lavishly built church was made in honour of St Francis, who championed the poor, was poor himself and did not value wealth.
- The priest (showing tourists around) concentrates on the decoration of the church and ignores the beggar outside.

Marks

Any three distinct points along the lines of the ones described above would be given three marks.

Answer

2 Show how the poet uses contrasting word choice in stanza one to make **one** of these concerns clear. (3 marks)

In a question about word choice make sure that you isolate specific words or expressions. Don't make a general comment because this will be given no credit.

Answers

- 'hands on backwards' and 'twisted (legs)' – suggests deformity.
- 'slumped' – suggests he's not upright or confident, and indicates a lack of care, that he's given up, been neglected.
- 'half-filled sack' – suggests neglected or not looked after.

Any one of the above would work as a contrast to:

- 'three tiers (of churches)' – lavish/excessive construction.
- 'honour (of)' – suggests care/respect.

Marks

One reference from either side of the contrast and a comment would be given three marks.

Answer

3 Explain the poet's use of tone in stanza two. (2 marks)

Tone is a tricky one. It involves the writer's relationship with the reader; the way he 'talks' to the reader. Think tone of voice – angry, sad, aggressive, ironic, sarcastic, and so on. In writing, tone comes across in the writer's use of language, in his choice of words. As we saw above, MacCaig, in this stanza, gives his reaction to the priest's explanation of the paintings in the church by Giotto. Rather than being wowed by the art, MacCaig gives a very understated, cool reaction: 'I understood the explanation / the explanation and / the cleverness.' It is almost as if he is not saying what he really thinks – he is being ironic, there might be some anger there. He understands that something is not right about a church that has lavish decoration, but has poor people suffering outside.

Answers

- Tone – irony, anger.
- Irony (and/or) anger comes across in MacCaig's use of the words 'understood' and 'cleverness' in the lines 'I understood / the explanation and / the cleverness.' ⇨

87

Marks

One mark for identification of tone.
One mark for example of use of tone.

Answer

4 Show how **two** examples of the poet's use of language in the final stanza effectively contribute to the main ideas or concerns of the poem. (4 marks)

To answer this question you should quote two examples from the final stanza and comment on them with reference to the main ideas of the poem. Look again at our discussion of the poem's ending on page 80. In a question like this you are given free choice. You are not directed to any part of the stanza, you just need to have the confidence to pick out a use of language, and to comment on it with reference to the main ideas of the poem.

Answers

- '(tourists), clucking contentedly' – word choice suggests the tourists behaving like birds, blindly/ironically following the priest and not the ideas of St Francis.
- 'contentedly' – this word suggests the tourists are self-satisfied and ignore the real issues of poverty/neglect that are present.
- 'fluttered' – this word suggests the frivolous behaviour of the tourists.
- 'clucking contentedly' – alliteration draws attention to the words (as above).
- 'as he scattered / the grain of the Word' – this image ironically compares the priest to Jesus (and possibly St Francis). Is MacCaig criticising the priest for spreading the wrong 'Word'? Again, the 'grain' suggests that the priest is feeding the tourists what they want to hear.
- 'ruined temple' – in this image the beggar is ironically compared to the lavish church. The church has been cared for, he has not. He is 'ruined'.
- 'eyes / wept pus,' 'lopsided mouth,' for example – word choice here emphasises the plight of the beggar and his need for care.
- 'said Grazie in a voice as sweet / as a child's' – this comparison of the beggar's voice to that of a child draws the reader's sympathy to the beggar, and links him further with St Francis.
- 'to St Francis' – ending the poem with the words 'St Francis' reminds the reader that it is St Francis, and his ideas, that the church is supposed to be celebrating.

Marks

Two examples of use of language plus two comments would mean four marks.

Answer

5 With close textual reference, show how a theme (or themes) from this poem has similarity with a theme (or themes) from at least one other poem by MacCaig that you have read. (8 marks)

In order to achieve full marks for this question you need to be able to identify a theme (or themes) from this poem and at least one other and explain this theme (or themes). You also need to make one reference to this poem and one reference to another which relates to these themes.

Themes

- Themes – 'Assisi' and 'Basking Shark' share themes – the value of experience, the human condition, what it means to be human, human imperfection.

Features

- Use of imagery/metaphors – both poems make use of strong imagery, for example, 'roomsized monster with a matchbox brain' from 'Basking Shark', and 'A rush of tourists, clucking contentedly,' from 'Assisi'.
- Word choice – both poems include careful use of words to communicate theme. (See answers above.)
- Alliteration – MacCaig uses alliteration to emphasise key words and expressions ('tiny twisted legs' and 'clucking contentedly' from 'Assisi', and 'monster with a matchbox brain' from 'Basking Shark').

Marks

In order to achieve full marks for this question, you must be able to identify a theme or themes from this poem and from at least one other. You will be given up to two marks for making this identification and explaining it.

You then have to make one reference to this poem (for example, to an idea, or to a technique which relates to a theme), and make a comment on it. This again is worth two marks (one mark for reference, one mark for comment).

To achieve the other four marks, you have to go on to make two further references to at least one other poem by MacCaig. You will be given one mark for each reference (for example, an idea, a technique or a relevant quote which relates to a theme), and one mark for each supporting comment.

This adds up to eight marks.

Remember

Your answer does not have to be a mini essay. You can answer in bullet points. The main thing to remember is: reference to text plus comment = two marks.

Key points !

In the Scottish Texts section of the Critical Reading paper you will always find a question from all writers on the published list of National 5 writers. One extract will be printed for each of the writers. The extract might be a complete poem (if it is a short poem), part of a longer poem, part of a short story, novel or play. If it is an extract from a poem or a short story, you will always be expected to make reference to at least one other poem or short story in the final question. However, if the extract is from a play or a novel, you will always be expected to make reference to at least one other part of the play or novel. The final question is always worth eight marks.

Ann Marie Di Mambro

We have looked at the Scottish poet Norman MacCaig and now we move on to drama with Ann Marie Di Mambro.

It is the purpose of this chapter to look at how *Tally's Blood* will work as an option in the Scottish texts section of the Critical Reading question paper. For this section, you are not thinking about essay preparation, you should be getting ready to answer questions on an extract from the play, and, in the last one of these questions, be ready to demonstrate your knowledge of the play as a whole. There are two broad skills areas that you have to develop here: your skills of analysis (as for RUAE), and your skills of knowledge and understanding (where you show what you have learned about a text, or texts, that you have studied).

The play *Tally's Blood* tells the story of an Italian immigrant family trying to build a life in Scotland around the time of the Second World War. Although it is set in the past, the issues raised by it are, of course, highly relevant to our times now: in the play, the Italian immigrants, and the Scottish people they meet, face many challenges and difficulties which affect their relationships. This is the essence of drama. Drama is all about conflict. There needs to be conflict for drama to work. In her introduction to the Hodder Gibson edition of the play, Ann Marie Di Mambro writes, 'Drama lies in what is going on between people at an emotional level.' There is certainly plenty of emotion expressed in *Tally's Blood*: love, hate, prejudice, loss, etc. From this list of emotions, several of the key themes of the play emerge too. All of the four mentioned above should certainly be on your revision list of the play's key themes.

When you are starting to think about the play, and are planning your revision for the exam, it is well worth reading Ann Marie Di Mambro's introduction to her play (as mentioned above). She writes about what she considers to be the important themes of the play: motherhood, prejudice, love, identity. Most of these themes centre around one of the main characters, Rosinella: she longs to be a mother, and brings up her niece, Lucia, as if she is her own daughter; she loves, and is loved by, Massimo; she displays great prejudice, and then learns from it. When you are revising a play, the themes are important, but character is important too. Themes often emerge from the words and actions of the main characters, and from their relationships with each other (often involving conflict).

Another important aspect of drama, again mentioned by Di Mambro, is setting. The play is largely set in the Pedreschi's café, a business set up by the Italian family as they try to settle and make a life and living in a new country – Scotland. It is here that the young people of the play, Lucia (from Italy), and Hughie (from Scotland), meet and fall in love. As their relationship develops we see the pressures and difficulties of living life as an immigrant. As a young girl, Lucia finds it difficult to accept Scottish culture: she insists on speaking Italian, and rejects the language spoken in Scotland. Rosinella shows prejudice when she makes it clear that she would not want Lucia to be involved with a Scottish boy. (She later regrets this, and helps bring them together.)

Key points

You are guaranteed one extract from the play *Tally's Blood* in the Scottish Texts section of the exam. The extract could come from anywhere in the play, so it is important that you prepare for this by becoming familiar with the play as a whole. You will not be asked to identify exactly where the extract has come from, but it will really help you in the exam if you are able to say to yourself, 'I know which part this is.' You will be asked three or four questions on the extract itself – these will be worth 12 marks in total. (Each one will be either two or four marks.) Then there is the final eight-mark question which asks you to show your knowledge of the whole play.

The final question

The final question (worth eight marks) will ask you to deal with one aspect of the extract and then to examine how this aspect works elsewhere in the play. You will be given up to two marks for your comments on the material given to you in the extract, a further two marks for general comments on the aspect identified, and then up to four marks for your analysis of the identified aspect from elsewhere in the play. For this last part of the question you need to be able to refer to material from at least one other part of the play.

Hints & tips ⭐

Analysis skills for plays

For an assessment on Tally's Blood you will be expected to do two different kinds of analysis:

✓ *Close analysis of the extract given to you in the exam paper. This is called 'textual analysis' and is very similar to the kind of exercise you have to do in the Reading for Understanding, Analysis and Evaluation section of the exam.*

✓ *Broader analysis from elsewhere in the play. This kind of analysis does not have to be as 'close' as the first kind. You might refer to other 'key episodes/ key events' (in other words, to things that happen, things that characters do) in the play. You might refer to examples of conflict or reconciliation, or to a character learning from an important event. You do not need to quote actual words from the play. In some circumstances a quote might back up your points neatly, but in this kind of analysis it is not essential, a 'reference' will do. For example, you could make a point of analysis about Rosinella's character by saying that she could be called a hypocrite when she is against Lucia having a choice in the boy that she wants to be with. Your evidence for this is when Rosinella tells Lucia that she had in fact defied her own parents by running away with Massimo so that she could be with him. You haven't quoted from the play here, but you have made 'reference' to it.*

Preparing for the final question on *Tally's Blood*

The final eight-mark question is where you are given the chance to show your knowledge and understanding of the whole play, in addition to your skills of analysis. Again, you have to do this from memory as you are not allowed to take the text into the exam room. With a play like *Tally's Blood* this is not as difficult as it sounds. The play is centred around a few main characters: Rosinella, Massimo, Lucia, Hughie, Bridget, Franco. You should aim to focus mainly on these characters (Rosinella and Massimo especially), and how they relate to each other. Then you can widen out your revision to other important aspects, such as theme and setting.

Activities ✏️

Building a timeline for Rosinella

One of the most useful preparations you can make is to compile a manageable timeline of the most important events for the main characters in the play. This is also good practice for one of the key National 5 English skills – identifying key points, or summary. It would be a good idea to start with Rosinella.

⇨

The character of Rosinella

Take a sheet of A4 paper and set it out as landscape. Draw a straight line across the middle of the page. Now, starting from the left, plot the main events for Rosinella along the line, like this:

Rosinella takes Lucia from Luigi (to Scotland)	Rosinella buys Lucia new party dress	Rosinella quizzes Franco about Luigi	Rosinella confronts Franco about Bridget

You might need a few sheets of paper to complete this task! If you end up with too much, try to cut it down to a workable amount. This, again, is useful because it is forcing you to make decisions about what to include and what to leave out. This is an important skill to master for National 5 English (and for all your exams).

Once you have a timeline that you are happy with, the next stage is to add comments of analysis under each entry. Something like this:

Rosinella takes Lucia from Luigi (to Scotland)	Rosinella buys Lucia new party dress	Rosinella quizzes Franco about Luigi	Rosinella confronts Franco about Bridget
Rosinella cares about Lucia. Massimo is loving/caring: 'puts an arm protectively round her shoulder'	Rosinella 'spoils' Lucia, but also really cares about her. Suggestion that Rosinella is unselfish as she doesn't buy herself a 'new coat.'	Rosinella worries about Luigi's role in Lucia's life – really cares about Lucia (but maybe becoming possessive, controlling). 'Did he ask about his lassie? ... I have to know everything.'	Rosinella shows her prejudice against Scottish girls – 'You're surely no keen on this Scotch girl.' Reveals bitterness about having no children of her own – 'It's no fair ... Twelve years I've been married and nothing. Me an Italian as well.'

Notice how I have added some actual quotations to the analysis sections. This will help you to select the most important quotes or references for use in the exam. As you go on with your timeline you could try to add in some notes about conflict with other characters. This will help you to think about the key relationships in the play. The first place to go for this might be Act One Scene Four where there is the first real conflict between Rosinella and her husband, Massimo. It follows on from the suggestion above that Rosinella might be spoiling Lucia …

Try to find the confidence to flick back and forward through the play, looking for important moments of conflict or character interest and jotting them down. If you go on in this way you will have a good set of notes to work with in preparation for the Scottish Texts section of the exam.

Rosinella

Prejudiced – 'These Scotch girls, they're all the same.' Theme of prejudice.

Hypocritical – tells Lucia 'we ran away' (meaning Massimo and her), but later says 'stay away from that Hughie Devlin, you hear'.

Suffers – 'There's too much heartache'.

Massimo

Loves Rosinella – 'That's ma heart Rosinella. And he's beating just for you.' Theme of love.

Forgiving – has a terrible experience during the war but wants to put that behind him and move on with his life. (Rosinella is more resentful.)

Identity issues – 'I always thought I was lucky. I had two countries. Now I feel I've got nowhere.' Theme of identity.

Notice that I have started to add in themes where they come up too.

Now you are ready to try a Scottish Texts assessment on *Tally's Blood*.

The extract below is taken from Act 2 Scene 5. Massimo is trying to tell Rosinella about a letter he has received from Luigi.

Tally's Blood

Massimo holds Rosinella firmly by her two arms.

MASSIMO: Rosie, I've had a letter from Luigi. He's sent for Lucia. She's to go home.

Silence: Rosinella horror-struck in disbelief: Massimo keeps hold of
5 *her, she stares at him.*

ROSINELLA: For a holiday?

MASSIMO: To live.

ROSINELLA: (*Mutters*) No...no...no...you're wrong...You're wrong...

10 MASSIMO: Rosie...

ROSINELLA: He can't...he can't do that to me...He can't do that...

MASSIMO: (*Looks at letter*) He says he can never repay us for all our kindness in looking after –

ROSINELLA: (*Interrupting/grabs letter*) Give me that.

15 *She scans letter but of course can't read it. Massimo continues*
without it.

⇨

⇨ MASSIMO: – all our kindness in looking after Lucia for him –

ROSINELLA: (*Angry*) 'Looking after?' – we brought her up. And I didn't do it for him. You tell him that. I did it for my sister.

20 MASSIMO: – he says he never wanted to be separated from her all these years, but what with the war –

ROSINELLA: Just what can HE give her? What, eh?

MASSIMO: – says he wants her to be with her brothers, who are all longing to meet her.

25 ROSINELLA: (*Scoffs*) He's got five sons and four walls. Hasn't even got a wall for each son!

MASSIMO: (*Gently admonishing*) Rosinella!

ROSINELLA: How can he do this?

MASSIMO: Rosie, please.

30 ROSINELLA: He thinks he can do this? He's daft. He must be daft.

MASSIMO: Rosie, will you listen please? You remember the night before we brought Lucia back. We sat up. Remember? We said we were frightened for just one thing. Loving a child that's not

35 your own is the hardest love of all. The more you love them, the more pain you get when they have to go back.

ROSINELLA: (*In disbelief*) That's nineteen years ago.

MASSIMO: I know. But we agreed then that we would be strong when it happened to us. We said we would be ready for it.

40 ROSINELLA: What? And you're ready for this, are you?

Massimo shakes his head, distraught.

MASSIMO: God, no.

ROSINELLA: Then stop being so bloody stupid!

Exam-style questions

1 Look again at lines 1–11.
   By referring to two examples of language, explain how the writer makes clear Rosinella's reaction to the contents of the letter. (4 marks)

2 Look again at lines 17–26.
   Using your own words as far as possible, identify two points Rosinella makes in disagreement with the contents of Luigi's letter. (2 marks)

3 Look again at lines 27–36.
   By referring to one example of language, explain how the writer makes it clear that Massimo is trying to calm Rosinella down. (2 marks)

4 Look again at lines 37–43.
   By referring to two examples of language, explain how the writer makes it clear that both Rosinella and Massimo have strong feelings at this point in the play. (4 marks)

5 By referring to this extract and to elsewhere in the play, show how an important theme is explored. (8 marks)

Answer

1 Look again at lines 1–11.
   By referring to two examples of language, explain how the writer makes clear Rosinella's reaction to the contents of the letter.
   (4 marks)

Answer

- 'Rosinella horror-struck' – this is from the stage directions and suggests that Rosinella is immediately filled with fear.
- 'in disbelief' – this is from the stage directions and suggests that Rosinella can't accept the news in the letter.
- 'she stares at him' – this is from the stage directions and suggests that Rosinella is in shock.
- 'For a holiday?' – this question suggests that Rosinella is trying to soften the news/make it more bearable.
- 'No…no…no…you're wrong…You're wrong …' or 'He can't … he can't' – the repetition suggests that Rosinella will not accept the news.

Marks

Two references plus two relevant comments would be given four marks.

Answer

2 Look again at lines 17–26.
   Using your own words as far as possible, identify two points Rosinella makes in disagreement with the contents of Luigi's letter.
   (2 marks)

This is a question which tests your understanding of a section of the extract. Here you are looking to pick out two negative points that Rosinella makes in response to things said by Luigi in the letter. Remember to write down these two points in your own words.

Answer

- Rosinella says that she raised Lucia/was a mother to her ('Looking after? – we brought her up.').
- Rosinella says she did not raise Lucia for Luigi's benefit ('And I didn't do it for him.').
- Rosinella says Luigi would be a poor parent for Lucia/wouldn't be able to offer Lucia anything ('Just what can HE give her?').
- Rosinella says Luigi can't afford/doesn't have the resources to look after Lucia (He's got five sons and four walls. Hasn't even got a wall for each son!').

Marks

One mark for each point made.

Answer

3 Look again at lines 27–36.

By referring to one example of language, explain how the writer makes it clear that Massimo is trying to calm Rosinella down. (2 marks)

For this question, you are looking for one example of language which helps to show that Massimo makes an effort to calm Rosinella.

You can choose any language feature you want: word choice, stage directions, sentence structure, etc. You can see below that there are plenty of options.

Answer

- '(Gently admonishing)' – stage directions suggest Massimo is trying to give Rosinella a bit of a row.
- 'Rosinella!' – the exclamation mark suggests that Massimo is trying to be firm by raising his voice for emphasis.
- 'Rosie, please' – this suggests patient pleading from Massimo.
- 'Rosie, will you listen please?' – question suggests that Massimo is trying to get Rosinella's attention. He is trying to reason with her.
- 'Remember?' – with this question Massimo is trying to get Rosinella to cast her mind back and focus on an agreement they made long ago.
- 'The more you love them, the more pain…' – these words suggest that Massimo is trying to reason with Rosinella.

Marks

One reference plus comment would be given two marks.

Answer

4 Look again at lines 37–43.

By referring to two examples of language, explain how the writer makes it clear that both Rosinella and Massimo have strong feelings at this point in the play. (4 marks)

The extract (and the scene) ends with a show of strong feelings from both Rosinella and Massimo. Here, you have to find two examples of language which make these strong feelings clear. Note that the question asks you to deal with both Rosinella and Massimo. So, you must find one example and comment for each.

Answer

Rosinella

'(In disbelief)' – this suggests that Rosinella is in shock.

'What? And you're ready for this, are you?' – suggests that Rosinella is strongly accusing Massimo.

'Then stop being so bloody stupid!' – the aggressive language here suggests that Rosinella is telling Massimo off.

⇨

Massimo

'Massimo shakes his head, distraught' – suggests that Massimo is very upset, confused by the implications of it all.

'God, no' – strong exclamation suggests that Massimo too is in shock, very upset.

Marks

Two references plus two relevant comments would be given four marks.

Hints & tips

Your answer does not have to be a mini essay. You can answer in bullet points. The main thing to remember is: reference to text plus comment = two marks.

Answer

5 By referring to this extract and to elsewhere in the play, show how an important theme is explored. (8 marks)

This is where you have the opportunity to show your knowledge of the play as a whole, and this is where your revision (timeline, mind maps, etc.) comes in. The question asks about an important theme, and in this example, you are given the freedom to choose the theme for yourself. The only thing to bear in mind when choosing a theme is that it must work with the extract.

Answer

In order to achieve full marks for this question, you must identify a theme that emerges in this extract, and then relate it to how the theme operates elsewhere in the play.

There should ideally be three parts to your answer, and they can be remembered as three words: commonality, extract, elsewhere.

1 Statement of identification of theme and how it relates to the play as a whole. (This is called commonality.)
2 Analysis of how the theme works in the extract (reference plus comment).
3 Analysis of two examples from elsewhere in the play, both showing how the theme works (reference plus comment times two).

Here is a worked example of how this approach might work:

An important theme from *Tally's Blood* is love. Massimo and Rosinella clearly love each other, but they come into conflict as the action of the play progresses, and their relationship looks to be under threat. Fortunately they realise how much they love each other by the end. In the extract Massimo says to Rosinella, 'But we agreed then that we would be strong when it happened to us.' This shows that Massimo and Rosinella did have a close bond, and that they were confident that their relationship would survive difficulties like this.

Later in the play Rosinella decides that she is unhappy and she tells Massimo she wants to leave Scotland. Massimo is furious with Rosinella and accuses her of being selfish '(*Voice breaks*) But you!

You never think of anyone but yourself.' The stage direction and the exclamation help to make clear Massimo's anger, and the fact that their love seems to have gone wrong.

At the end of the play, as a result of the part that Rosinella plays in bringing Lucia and Hughie together, Rosinella and Massimo realise that they do in fact truly love each other. This is made clear in Massimo's words, 'That's ma heart, Rosie. And he's beating just for you.'

Marks

The worked example above would be given eight marks: two marks for commonality, two for the example from the extract, four from elsewhere (two examples plus two comments).

Tally's Blood

Ann Marie Di Mambro

HODDER
GIBSON
LEARN MORE

Frequently asked questions

English is not my best subject, but I need a good mark in it. What should I do?

The first thing is – try to get into it and try to stay interested. The worst thing you can do is to give up and lose interest. If this happens, you will probably end up just looking over a few notes before the exam and hoping for the best. You are unlikely to do well in these circumstances. You will get much more out of English, and achieve a better result, if you can maintain some level of interest. Keep involved. It is perfectly possible to learn the skills required to do well in English; you do not need some kind of magic touch, or special talent. If you follow the advice of your teacher (and this book!), you will be fine. You are at an advantage with the subject called English because it covers the language you use every day (and may well have been using all your life). However, you do need to learn and develop a set of skills. A lot of these skills centre on reading: it is a simple fact that doing some reading will improve your skills in English (even if you don't realise it!). If you can't get into reading novels, or longer books, try others kinds of text such as newspapers and magazines. Any reading will help!

Does spelling matter?

The short answer is: in the Portfolio and the Critical Essay, yes but in the Reading for Understanding paper, and in the Scottish Texts section, no.

When you are working on your Portfolio, aim for zero errors in your spelling, grammar and sentence construction. This should not be a problem as you have the opportunity to re-draft your work.

However, you have to write your Critical Essay first-draft under exam conditions. Do your best to keep an eye on the technical accuracy of your writing. Don't let this put you off and spoil your essay, though. You are looking for your writing to be 'consistently accurate'. This does not mean that the accuracy has to be perfect, but it cannot be full of mistakes.

Is spelling the most common problem with technical accuracy?

No, the most common error is what is known as 'comma splice'. This is when you put a comma instead of a full stop. Watch out for this. When in doubt, make it a full stop.

What if there are some words in the exam that I don't know the meaning of?

The main thing is – don't let this put you off. If you look at the surrounding words there are usually clues to the meaning of a difficult, or unusual, word. It is unlikely that you will be asked a direct question about a really tricky word.

How long should I spend on each question?

You have an hour in total to complete the Reading for Understanding, Analysis and Evaluation paper. Use the first ten minutes to read the passage carefully, this leaves you with 5 or 6 minutes to spend on each question.

The Critical Reading paper is 1 hour and 30 minutes long. You should spend 45 minutes on each of the two tasks. It is not a good idea to take longer on one than the other. You may think that you could finish one quickly, but it often doesn't work out like that, and you can end up not finishing something.

What if I run out of time, and I don't finish my essay?

This depends. If you are running out of time and think that you might not finish it, you should try to end it in some way – add a conclusion. It is better to submit an essay that is rounded off in some way than one that just stops. A concluded essay (even it is concluded clumsily) will get a better mark than one that is left unfinished.

In class we have studied two of the specified Scottish writers. Can I use one for the Scottish Texts section, and the other one for the Critical Essay?

Yes. But they can't both be from the same genre (type), so you couldn't use two from Prose, or two from Drama, or two from Poetry. In other words, you couldn't use Norman MacCaig for the Scottish Texts section, and Carol Ann Duffy for the Critical Essay.

Do I have to learn quotes for the Critical Essay?

Yes! However, actual quotes are much more significant/necessary for essays on Drama or Poetry texts. For Prose (especially novels), quotes are not so significant. If you are writing about a novel you will be dealing primarily with key episodes and characterisation and therefore direct quotations are not so significant. But, if you are writing about a poem you will need to use actual quotation – if it is a reasonably short poem, try to learn it by heart! If you are writing about a character in a play, you will be referring to his/her actions and his/her words. You will need to remember some significant quotes in order to do this.

In this book, you talk about 'quotes' and 'references to the text'. Are these the same thing?

A quote contains the exact words that appear in a text. A reference could be a summary of what someone has said, a re-telling of an important event in a novel, and so on. In the Scottish Texts section a quote OR a reference is usually worth one mark, and a related comment is worth one mark.

I have lots of notes on my main text for the Critical Essay. How can I possibly remember them all?

You won't and you can't. Try to condense your notes down into what you think are the most important things. Try to group material on the same subject – put all the stuff about the ending together, all the notes about the themes together, and so on. Then re-write your notes. As you get closer to the exam, try to be working with as little paper as possible. Make these sheets of paper as easy to read, and as eye-catching as possible. Use different colours of pen. Underline or highlight important words. If you know you are just looking at a few sheets of paper in the last few days before the exam you will feel much more confident about learning the material. It won't seem so off-putting.

Everyone says my handwriting is awful. Should I be worried?

Everyone says that about mine! I don't worry about it because usually no one really needs to read what I write by hand. However, if I have to write for an audience, I try to write a bit more clearly. That's the main thing to consider – someone has to be able to read your essay. If the marker can read it (and they do try hard to do this), there is no problem. If you are really concerned about a marker being able to read your work, then speak to your teacher to see what arrangements can be made.

I know that I have to revise for the Critical Essay and the Scottish Texts, but how do I prepare for the Reading for Understanding, Analysis and Evaluation exam?

The main thing here is practice. Do the questions in Chapter 4 of this book, and look carefully at the answers. Read as much as you can. (Read articles from the newspapers suggested in Chapter 1 as exam passages are often taken from these newspapers.) Revise the techniques used by writers (many of these are in the 'Remember' panels throughout this book).

Do you have any last minute advice for the exam?

Try to approach it as calmly as you can. (Remember the old football manager's saying 'A nervous player is not a good player'.) Work steadily through the papers, keeping an eye on the time so that you don't spend too long on one part. Remember that there is time built into the exam for you to read the passages. Don't be put off if people around you are scribbling away while you are still reading – it is better to proceed with understanding.

In the Reading for Understanding, Analysis and Evaluation paper remember to use your own words when the question asks for this.

In the Critical Essay, try to answer the specific question set. Keep your points as relevant as possible to the question.

In the Scottish Texts section remember that marks are often awarded in this way: quote/reference to the text is worth one mark, comment on the quote/reference is worth another mark.

Bring more than two pens, and make sure there is absolutely no chance that your 'phone will make any sound whatsoever!

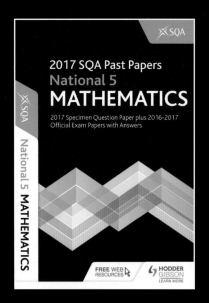
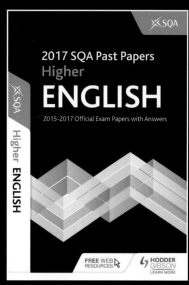
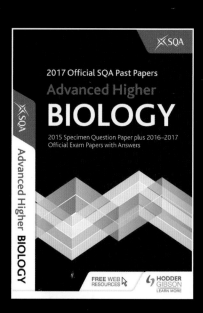